TRACKING THE HOLOCAUST

TRACKING THE
HOLOCAUST

Gerda Haas

ᚱP
RUNESTONE PRESS
THE LERNER GROUP
MINNEAPOLIS

RUNESTONE PRESS • ᚱᚢᚾᛖᛋᛏᛟᚾᛖ

rune (rōōn) *n* **1 a :** one of the earliest written alphabets used in northern Europe, dating back to A.D. 200; **b :** an alphabet character believed to have magic powers; **c :** a charm; **d :** an Old Norse or Finnish poem. **2 :** a poem or incantation of mysterious significance, often carved in stone.

Runestone Press
a division of Lerner Publications Company
241 First Avenue North
Minneapolis, MN 55401

Library of Congress Cataloging-in-Publication Data

Haas, Gerda (Gerda Schild)
[These I do remember]
Tracking the Holocaust / by Gerda Haas.
p. cm.
Previously published: These I do Remember. Freeport, Me. :
Cumberland Press, © 1982.
Includes bibliographical references and index.
ISBN 0-8225-3157-7
1. Holocaust, Jewish (1939–1945) — Juvenile literature.
[1. Holocaust, Jewish (1939–1945) I. Title.
D804.3.H319 1995
940.53'18—dc20 94-46003
CIP
AC

Manufactured in the United States of America
1 2 3 4 5 6 - JR - 99 98 97 96 95

In Memory of My Family

My mother, Paula Jochsberger Schild

ברײנדל בת גבריאל

My sister, Elfriede Schild

חוה בת ישראל

My husband's sister, Paula Haas Meyer

ברײנדל בת יהודה הלוי

Her daughters, Margot & Inge

&

My husband's sister, Erna Haas Weinstock

חוה בת יהודה הלוי

Her children Kurt, Ruth, Claude and Micheline

Let the martyrology from the Yom Kippur service be their epitaph

אלה אזכרה ונפשי עלי אשפכה

These I do remember. And my soul grieveth.
All through the age hatred hath pursued us.
Throughout the years ignorance hath devoured our martyrs.
As in one long day of blood. Rulers have risen through the endless years
Oppressive, savage in their witless power.
Filled with futile thought: To make an end to that which
God hath cherished.

Contents

Leningrad

RUSSIA

•
Moscow

•Minsk

**WHITE
RUSSIA**

• Babi Yar

Kiev•

UKRAINE

sy

ANIA

st

BLACK SEA

ARIA

TURKEY

IA

IA

EUROPE

During the Holocaust

Key	
•	City
✶	Ghetto
▬	Transit Camp
▲	Concentration Camp
☆	Death Camp

Shaded area is Nazi-occupied

Preface

Hitler had been dead for a year less three days when I stepped down the ramp of the S.S. *Mulholland* at Boston Harbor. Behind me were 12 years of oppression, 6 of those 12 spent in wartime and two of the 6 war years in a concentration camp. Behind me war criminals were being judged in Germany, and bombed cities were being rebuilt all over Europe from Poland to the Netherlands, from Italy to England. Before me was New England, America. The date was April 27, 1946; I was 23 years old.

How different my four children's youth has been from mine; how difficult for them to understand my story. They know bombing and killing and fear only vicariously, and when I tell them fragments of my experience in the war and in the Holocaust, they do not comprehend. And yet they must understand, must know how my life has been influenced by the system under which I lived. Perhaps they will then be better able to appreciate the freedom they enjoy and the society they live in.

I first began to realize that my American-born children took for granted the privileges which, for me, were so amazing, on a day in September 1977. At that point I had already been successful in completing the formal education that was interrupted in my youth: I had graduated from Bates College in 1971, from the University of Maine Graduate School in 1974 and was by then catalog librarian at Bates College; I had already served once on jury duty; I voted conscientiously and proudly at every chance; my family and I freely practiced the Jewish orthodox religion in Lewiston, Maine. Life, liberty and the pursuit of happiness had become a reality, and the oppressed past was history, however real. Then, in late summer of 1977, Governor James B. Longley nominated me for membership on the Maine State Board of Education. My children, by then all in their 20s, and my husband shared my excitement and the sense of honor over the Governor's nomination. But when the official letter arrived notifying me of my confirmation hearing before the Education Committee of the Senate, my heart sank: the date for the hearing was September 14, the second day of Rosh Hashanah, the Jewish New Year. I knew I could not travel to Augusta on the High Holiday.

With immeasurable regret that this honor and opportunity would now slip through my fingers, and with a deeply imprinted fear of approaching government, I called the chairman of the Education Committee and explained my dilemma to him, certainly not expecting the Committee to accommodate me. Warmth spread through me when he invited me to come for my hearing the following day. He assured me that the Education Committee would not mind meeting especially for that purpose.

I told my children about the phone call, but they seemed curiously unaffected by my excitement. One of my daughters said: "Why do you think that's so special, Mom?" She seemed to expect that the Committee would routinely reschedule the hearing if I could not attend because of the Jewish holiday. Her reaction was so different from mine that I was startled. The stark contrast in our very different expectations caused me to consider why our views were so different. That very evening I went to the basement and looked for the notes I had taken in 1945 after my liberation from concentration camp. I knew then that it was time to translate those yellowing pages. I knew that it was time to tell my children, and perhaps others brought up in a free society, what it was like to have lived under Hitler's Third Reich.

But even as I was translating my experiences, I began to understand two things: For one, my story was incomprehensible to my children without some sense of the history in which it occurred, and therefore I knew that I should write about Hitler's rise to power and the ensuing war, however briefly. The other thing I realized was that just one story—whether it was mine or another's, even when told in historical perspective—could not possibly give a sense of the range and variety of experiences, the depth of human suffering that was endured during the Holocaust years. I resolved to add Holocaust accounts from other European countries to my story and to tell them also in the context of their history. To add an account of every country that came under Hitler's domination seemed unnecessary for my purpose, and so I looked for only seven other examples besides mine. My intention is to show eight lives changed by history; to show history borne on the shoulders of eight of us: fragments picked from the millions of shattered lives.

I became aware of many such fragments in my library work. Book after book on the Holocaust crossed my desk: memoirs, biographies, diaries, firsthand reports of both Jewish and non-Jewish observers. At the same time, I read works on the history of the Third Reich and the Holocaust. Slowly my book took form.

I wanted to present human experience in historical context and impress the reader with the geographical range of the Holocaust. All this I wanted to include in my book and convey to my children and, by extension, to children of new generations who may regard the Holocaust as remote and difficult to understand.

As my book took shape, a sense of urgency claimed me. Since nearly the whole of Jewish youth under 18 was killed, the few of us who have survived, the men and women who are now in our late 70s and older, have a special responsibility: to share what we know and have experienced in the Holocaust. This responsibility, this awareness is my justification for telling this story, for writing this book.

Gerda Haas

Introduction

From 1933 to 1945, Germany was dominated by Adolf Hitler. Among the many Nazi laws and regulations that governed the country during those years, three are of importance here. The Racial Laws of September 15, 1935, which declared Jews stateless, unprotected by German law; the Gestapo Decree of April 15, 1940, which permitted the Gestapo to function outside of German law; and the guidelines of the Wannsee Conference of January 20, 1942, which gave the blueprint for the Final Solution to the Jewish question. Namely, all Jews were to be shipped to concentration camps; Jews under age 18 and over 45 would receive "special treatment" (treatment that turned out to be gassing and burning on arrival); and all others could expect hard labor, planned starvation, and eventual death. Therefore, in Germany and in German-occupied countries it was legal to kill Jews as enemies of the Reich. As a result, 6 million Jews, so-called enemies of Hitler's Third Reich, were legally gassed, burned, gunned into pits or otherwise slaughtered—an unprecedented event that we now call the Holocaust.

The Holocaust did happen, even though there were bystanders who claimed not to see or hear a thing. It happened even though there are Americans who still deny it. It happened even though there are young adults both in Europe and in the United States who don't believe it.

We, the last of the survivors, remember it all too well. We who were in our early 20s when we entered the camps and therefore were not immediately gassed—we are the last eyewitnesses to the Holocaust. This puts a unique duty upon our shoulders: We must talk about the Holocaust to the last days of our lives. We must explain the unexplainable, give the unspeakable words, and tell the world that the Holocaust is true, all too true. I am grateful to Lerner Publications and especially to one of my editors, Sandra Davis, for giving me this opportunity.

This book is a shorter version of my earlier book *These I Do Remember: Fragments from the Holocaust* (Cumberland Press, 1983). History is carried on the shoulders of real people, and conversely, people's experiences become clearer when told in the context of history. Therefore, I follow Hitler's armies on their amazing course through Europe, stopping eight times to tell of the German invasion's effects on a real person in a particular country.

The first story is my own, but it could be the story of a thousand young Jewish women living in Germany during the Nazi years—except I was luckier than most. I survived, came to the United States, married, brought up four children and to date we have eight grandchildren. Leesha Rose, survivor from Holland, also married, has a family and now lives in Israel. Fania Fenelon of France survived Auschwitz and continued her singing career. She died a few years ago. While all Jews were victims, not all victims were Jewish. Alys Stanké, a Catholic from Lithuania, now Alain, became a writer and publisher and lives in Canada. Isabella Leitner, survivor of Auschwitz and the Death March, lives in New York with her husband and family. Bryna Bar Oni came to the United States as well, but I don't know what became of her. As for the fate of the Nazis mentioned in this book, a section on their sentences at the end of the book can be consulted.

The Beginning of Nazi Rule in Germany

The *National Sozialistische Deutsche Arbeiterpartei*, the Nazi Party of Germany, was in power from 1933 to 1945. Twelve years: a short span in terms of time, a very long time in terms of human suffering. The Party became both the vehicle that carried Adolf Hitler to power and the instrument by which he ruled. In 1921, when he assumed Party leadership, he proclaimed to its few members that he intended to create a Third Reich for the German people in Europe, a Reich greater than either Charlemagne's First Reich of the ninth century or Bismarck's Second Reich of 1871-1918. His Reich, he promised, would last a thousand years and would bring a New Order to all of Europe. No German would live under the Soviet Star or the Star of David; all would be brought into the Reich. Over this new state would fly the symbol of German labor, the swastika. The New Order would make the Aryan race in Europe masters over the Slavic people. The Jews, he prophesied, would disappear. The Party granted him unlimited power.

By 1930, his brownshirted storm troopers, the *Sturm-abteilung,* or SA, marched by the thousands under the swastika banner, singing, "Today we rule Germany, tomorrow the world."

On January 30, 1933, President Hindenburg appointed Hitler Chancellor of Germany. Eighteen months later, Hindenburg died and Hitler abolished the post of president in the Reich. He was master in Germany now, absolute leader of the nation, the *Fuehrer.* He claimed his word as the voice of the German *Volk* (people) and that his will was their will. His word was indeed the law of the land, the only law. He was a man with unchecked power.

From the beginning of his dictatorship to the very end, Hitler proclaimed two doctrines above all others, two concepts that he fused into a twisted theme of war and murder. One was the *Lebensraum* doctrine—his claim that Germany needed more space in Europe. The other was *die Judenfrage* (the Jewish Question)—the question of how to get rid of the Jews. And as Hitler overpowered country after country throughout Europe, first in frightening takeovers, then in bloody wars, he simultaneously gained Lebensraum and eliminated Jews.

Lebensraum

Hitler claimed that Germany was without sufficient territory for living space and food production. Seventy million Germans were forced to live at a ratio of 140 persons to a square kilometer (.6 miles). This injustice, he declared, had been imposed on them by the terms of the Versailles Treaty of 1919. He declared that this treaty—created after Germany lost World War I—was the work of international Jewry and therefore criminal and invalid.

He defiantly marched his army into the Rhineland and annexed the borderlands which were inhabited by Germans: the Saar, Austria, the Memel Region, Sudetenland, and the Free City of Danzig. In March 1939, he seized Czechoslovakia, a country which was not inhabited by Germans. Now, he said, he had no further land claims to make in Europe.

Just six months later, in September 1939, Hitler broke his word and conquered Poland in a bloody war. He ordered Poles driven out of their homes and Poland be resettled with Germans. He then declared Poland a part of the German Reich. By employing this process again and again, he expected to justify his stampede through Europe: the attacks on Denmark, Norway, Holland, Belgium, Luxembourg and France; the violation of the Balkans; the devastation of Lithuania, the Ukraine and parts of Russia; the corruption of Italy and Hungary. The Lebensraum motive became World War II. The New Order was beginning to be implemented: Men and women of Europe were shipped to the Reich for slave labor, and Jews all over Europe were killed.

The Jewish Question

The Jews are our misfortune! screamed anti-Jewish posters in all languages, rekindling old hatred. Jew-hatred in Europe was as old as Jewish history, unchanged except for the name: In the 19th century, in search of a better term, the expression *anti-Semitism* was introduced.

Hitler legalized anti-Semitism by means of the Nüremberg Laws of September 15, 1935. These laws decreed that only Aryans (defined as anyone with four German grandparents) could be citizens of the Reich. The Nüremberg Laws forbade marriage between Aryans and Jews. Sexual relations between the two races became a criminal offense. The same laws proclaimed the swastika the official national symbol. Only citizens of the Reich were allowed to display it. The Jews were now unprotected by German law. Over the next seven years, more laws to isolate and disinherit the Jews were put into effect. The laws sent Jews to ghettos and concentration camps, and ultimately decreed their murder.

By late 1938, Jews in small towns and villages had to sell their properties to the Germans for a fraction of their real value and move to larger cities. Three years later, in November 1941, a new law said that "Jews who take up residence abroad" were no longer Reich nationals and the Reich could confiscate their property and possessions. It sounded so civilized. But in reality, Jews were being forced out of Germany, deported beyond the borders of the Reich into occupied territory, penned inside ghettos and concentration camps, while the German state stole their wealth.

To confine the Jews to a designated area within a large town or city was not an original idea. Historically, ghettos had been quarters of the city where Jews could feel safe from harassment, move about freely, and prosper. In the ghettos of the Middle Ages, the Jewish heritage flourished. Religious and social unity gave strength and togetherness to the ghetto inhabitants. Inside their ghetto walls, medieval Jews preserved a unique custom of dress. Sometimes, to mark them as separate, they were forced to wear a Jewish star or a peculiar kind of "Jew hat." With the growing liberalism of the 18th century, ghetto gates opened and walls tumbled. This happened first in France, then spread through all of Europe. Restrictions ended. Marks on clothing were disregarded—until September 19, 1941.

From that day on, all persons defined as Jews by the Nüremberg Laws had to wear the Yellow Star of David with the word *Jude, Jood,* or *Juif* printed in its center in large, black, Hebrew-type letters. Thus labeled, the Jews of Europe were herded into Nazi-constructed ghettos in all towns and cities on the occupied Continent. Once there, the Jews were ordered to govern themselves through Jewish councils headed by a Jewish Elder. These powerless administrators were completely dominated by the SS—the German elite storm troopers.

Though these modern ghettos concentrated the Jewish population, they were not the solution the Nazis wanted to the Jewish problem. For this, the Nazis used concentration camps. The first such concentration camp was Dachau, near Munich, established in 1933. Others sprang up: Buchenwald near Weimar; Sachsenhausen and Oranienburg near Berlin; Mauthausen near Linz in Austria. After the conquest of Poland, sinister camp complexes were built in the East: Auschwitz, Belzec, Maidanek, Treblinka. Their number grew until there were some 30 of them on the map of the Reich and its territories. What was their purpose? What were the Gestapo (Nazi secret police) and the SS gearing up for?

The Gestapo Empire

The Gestapo had initially been created to act as an instrument of terror within the Nazi Party—just as the feared SS was at first nothing more than Hitler's bodyguard. But both organizations quickly grew into one powerful German police force, whose business was the destruction of the Jews. In June 1934, Heinrich Himmler became chief of the SS and all other German police. The Gestapo's division for Jewish Affairs was considered very important and had offices in Berlin, headed by Heinrich Müller and Adolf Eichmann. When Hitler gave Himmler full authority over the Jews in Germany and the occupied territories, orders passed from him through Reinhard Heydrich (later Ernst Kaltenbrunner) to Müller and Eichmann, and from them to the inspector of concentration camps, Moss, and through him to all camp commanders.

In February 1936, the German Supreme Court passed a law prohibiting interference with Gestapo activities, especially in actions against Jews. The Gestapo was the law. In January 1942, Gestapo and SS officers and selected officials of the Reich and the occupied Eastern territories met at Heydrich's invitation. At Wannsee, near Berlin, they discussed the complete solution of the Jewish question. Unrestrained by German law, these men devised the last step, the "Final Solution" to the Jewish problem—annihilating the Jews in Polish concentration camps. In their official documents they used guarded language such as "evacuation to the East" and "special treatment," but in effect this meant cattle cars for transporting their victims, gas chambers for murdering them, and ovens for the disposal of millions of bodies. To prevent rebellion, the Jews were told that they were being resettled in labor camps where they were needed to work. So that no one would question what use old and sick Jews and permanently disabled veterans of World War I might be in labor camps, a ghetto was set up in Czechoslovakia at Theresienstadt for Jews over 65, disabled war veterans, partners of mixed marriages, and their children. Internationally known Jewish scientists and artists could also be sent to this ghetto, (which the Nazis thought of as "privileged") in case the free world should inquire about them.

Did the World Know the Awful Truth?

Did world leaders care or help? In July 1938, President Roosevelt called a conference at Èvian on the French shore of Lake Geneva. Representatives of 32 countries met to discuss ways to help the Jews of Europe. An international refugee committee was formed, with headquarters in London. The group claimed the right to speak out for the Jews, which might have been beneficial, except that it was never heard from. As the situation worsened, each unoccupied country acted—or did not act—on its own. A few world figures spoke out. Most were silent.

In Europe, England's borders were open to Jews. Sweden harbored and saved the Danish Jews, and all others who could reach Swedish shores. Portugal acted as a stepping-stone to freedom. The south of France protected thousands of fugitives before the Nazi occupation of that area. Switzerland granted temporary refuge to hundreds of fleeing families during the early years of Nazi Germany. In 1936 the Swiss chief of police, Dr. Heinrich Rothmund, requested that the Germans stamp Jewish passports with a visible "J." From then on, Swiss border police were instructed to turn Jewish fugitives back to the German authorities. Fortunately, the border police ignored the J-stamped passports and allowed many Jews to slip through. Swiss borders again opened wide in 1944 and 1945, when Himmler agreed to release Jews in exchange for American money. Concentration camp survivors found hospitality in Swiss refugee camps until they could arrange their emigration to America or Palestine.

The United States did not alter its immigration policies, which were based on an old quota system—a set number of immigrants from each country were accepted in the United States each year. The Jews of Europe, yearning for the freedom of the United States, had to wait their turn and then could only get visas if they could prove that they would be able to support themselves. Poverty-stricken Polish Jews were left out. Even Palestine was not open to them. Palestine, under British rule, restricted Jewish immigration to wealthy Jews and Jewish farmers who could help build the land. In this way the British hoped to appease the Arabs, knowing how they hated Jews.

Cuba accepted the fleeing Jews but only on a temporary basis while awaiting their quota entry to the United States. Shanghai took in thousands of Jews, but it was a long way from Europe. Australia, South Africa and South America granted refuge, but few could afford the expense of emigration visas and long journeys. With no haven in reach, millions of Jews were at the mercy of the Nazi hunters.

By mid-1942, President Roosevelt knew about the mass killings in Germany and Poland. He spoke out publicly and strongly but did nothing more than that. The Pope—Pius XII—was asked to make a similar statement, but declined. When the Nazis occupied Italy in 1943 and began rounding up Jews in the streets of Rome, the Pope ordered the Vatican's convents and monasteries to take in and shelter as many Jews as they could hold. At that late date he saved thousands of lives. In July 1944, Anthony Eden, foreign minister of England, received a letter from

Chaim Weizmann, a leader in the creation of the Jewish state and later, Israel's first president. Weizmann asked for England's Royal Air Force to bomb both the notorious death camps of Auschwitz and Birkenau and the railroad lines leading to them. The answer, received a month later, was no. The project could not be pursued due to so-called technical difficulties. The Jews of Europe were doomed to wait behind barbed wire until the liberators arrived.

World Highlights, 1930-1935

The planet Pluto is discovered by astronomers at the Lowell Observatory. Comic strip "Blondie" becomes popular. The Empire State Building is completed. Gandhi is arrested. Aldous Huxley writes Brave New World. *Lindbergh baby is kidnapped. Amelia Earhart is the first woman to fly solo across the Atlantic Ocean. Sophia Loren is born. Harold Urey is awarded the Nobel Prize for his discovery of heavy hydrogen. The Dionne quintuplets are born. Franklin D. Roosevelt becomes president of the United States and the New Deal evolves. Albert Einstein leaves Germany for America. Persia changes its name to Iran.*

Growing up in Germany: Gerda's Story

When Hitler came to power in 1933, I was 10 years old. I lived in Ansbach, a small, romantic town near Nürem-berg in southern Germany. I lived in a big brick house with my mother, father, sister, Friedl, and grandmother. Father's kosher butcher shop was in the front of the house; we lived in back and upstairs, even in the attic. Under the slanting roof and the high mansard windows, Friedl and I had a spacious, sunny playroom. We could prop up the windows and, standing on tiptoes, look out at a large part of town. I loved seeing the railroad tracks and watching the trains toot by. Or, looking up, we gaped at the few airplanes that announced themselves with lots of rumbling noise. But our undivided interest was spent watching the activities in the untidy stork nest on the chimney of a neighboring roof. Our parents' anxious discussions in the rooms below us did not yet darken our sunny childhood.

Soon there were things to watch right from the living room windows. Every day and many nights, brownshirted marchers in tight formation made the cobblestones clank as they marched down the street carrying flags and banners, singing loudly of Germany's glory and the Jews' dishonor. At night they lit up the streets with torchlight parades. We watched in awe and listened in fear. We put our ears to the keyhole, listening as our parents and grandmother speculated on what the future might bring for us all. We also listened to Hitler's speeches on our Blaupunkt radio, but we couldn't make any sense out of his thundering promise to create a new Thousand-Year Reich that would be free of Jews.

Gradually, our lives changed. Neighbors, once friendly,

now looked away when they saw us. Other children stopped walking to school with us. By 1936, Friedl and I were dismissed from school. A new law stated that German children could not sit in the same room with Jewish children. So, we had to leave. Friedl went to a Jewish agricultural school and I was sent to Berlin to attend a Jewish high school there. Berlin? That was 450 kilometers away. Who did I know there? Where would I live? I was 15 years old when I left home in the spring of 1938.

On November 12, I was suddenly called home. A few days earlier, a young Jew in Paris had read in a French newspaper that terrible atrocities had been committed against thousands of Jews in the Polish town of Zbonszyn. Suspecting that his own family was among them, he stormed into the German embassy in Paris and shot the German diplomat Ernst von Rath. The Nazis reacted to that impulsive act with fury. All through the night of November 9, all the next day and into the night of November 10, the SA and SS invaded the streets of every German city and town, smashing Jewish property, burning synagogues, and abusing hundreds of innocent Jewish men. In Ansbach, during the night, the SA collected the Jews from their homes and imprisoned them in a large meeting hall at the edge of town. From there, the men were sent to Dachau, but women and children were sent home in the morning with the command to "sell" their houses and businesses to waiting party members and to get out of Ansbach before the end of the year—or they would never see their men again. When I arrived home, my mother, grandmother, and Friedl were packing. We could only take what we were able to carry. But where would we go?

A month later, on a cold, snowy day, we shouldered our belongings and walked the few blocks to the railroad station. I couldn't bear to look back, to cast one more glance at the stately old house where I was born. I didn't dare look at my mother or sister either, knowing the agony in their souls. I looked straight ahead, hoping that our relatives in Munich would be able to take us in.

Father found us in Munich and now my parents made serious plans for the future. In August 1939, Father was able to go to England with a transport of Jewish men and boys. The plan was that he would find British families who would take Mother, Friedl and me in as "domestics." But a month after we had said a hopeful *auf Wiedersehen* to our papa, the war in Poland started and the borders to England were closed.

Mother, determined that we should live a useful life, sent Friedl to Frankfurt for nurses' training at a Jewish hospital. I went back to Berlin to train as a pediatric nurse. Mother claimed she didn't mind being all alone in Munich, but I knew better. She had never been alone in her life, had never had to make an independent decision. Munich was completely strange to her, a place where she had no friends, and now, not even her own family. We wrote her letters and called her as long as Jews were allowed to have telephones, and she wrote to us and called us. But the noose was tightening. From September 1941 on, Jews had to wear brightly visible yellow stars with the word Jude (Jew) printed on them in large black Hebrew-type letters. In October Jews began to be deported in horrible cattle cars to uncertain destinations, to be "resettled" and to do "war labor" in the East. When Mother was notified in November that she was to go into one of those resettlement transports to Riga, we actually believed the German lies. My sister even volunteered to go with her. We thought we'd all be reunited when my time came to be deported.

Theresienstadt

My time came in the evening of May 17, 1943, when SS men came to the Jewish Hospital in Berlin where I worked. The Nazis rounded up doctors, nurses, patients, even several children, for resettlement. The years in Berlin had been so stressful and deportation so certain that when it finally happened I was somehow relieved. I thought that I would see my mother and sister again. Together we could endure to the end of the war and then find our father. I took my packed backpack and willingly went into the waiting truck.

Incredibly, the truck stopped at Collection Center Gerlach Strasse which was used for Theresienstadt transports. Were we going to the "privileged" camp, Ghetto Theresienstadt, created for elite Jews, created to show the world how well Hitler treated the Jews? But I was not prominent. How did I rate a ticket to that place? "We are lucky," whispered an official of the Berlin Jewish Community Council, himself now a deportee. "There was a new directive from SS Headquarters just recently that Community personnel be shipped there instead of Auschwitz, at least for now." I stayed close to the children from our hospital and helped make them comfortable. On May 20, 1943, we were driven to a small side station, herded into waiting third-class railroad cars and left Berlin.

We came to a halt a day later at a country railroad station. The sign on the platform read: *Bauschowitz.*

Gerda Schild, 1936

Ansbach, Germany—Gerda's birthplace

Paula Schild, Gerda's mother. This photo was taken in 1940, after Gerda's father had to leave Germany.

Friedl Schild, Gerda's sister, in 1936.

*Gerda's parents,
Siegfried and Paula
Schild, reunited after
Siegfried's release from
prison in 1938.*

*Gerda's third grade class, 1928. Gerda is in the back row, fourth
from the right.*

Gerda's Jewish youth group in Ansbach, 1938. Gerda is third from the left and her sister, Friedl, is second from the right. Of this entire group, only four survived the Holocaust.

Sophie Jochsberger, Gerda's grandmother, in 1930.

Gerda's sister (far right) and friends—the last picture taken before they had to leave Ansbach, about 1938.

Ghetto money in Theresienstadt in Kronen, *Czech currency*

Gerda in Switzerland, 1945.

The nurse's pin Gerda wore in Berlin. It reads "Jewish Home for Babies."

*Gerda's friend from Theresienstadt, Eva Hammel (back, standing)
with the family they now share. From left: Sarah, Rafi, Benjamin,
and Jonathan Hammel, and their parents, Eva's son Jean and
Gerda's daughter Polly.*

*Gerda's extended family, Minneapolis, 1992: Front, left to right:
Rudolph Haas, Sarah Hammel, Ari David, Rafi Hammel, Gerda
Haas holding Margot Haas. Back, left to right: Benjamin Hammel,
Jonathan Hammel, Polly Haas-Hammel, Hedy Haas-David
holding Tali David, Bill David holding Rachel David, Leonard
Haas, Abby Gottsegen-Haas.*

The beautiful baroque synagogue of Ansbach, Germany, was built in 1745. Because it was surrounded by German houses, it was not burned down on Kristallnacht *and is now a memorial to the lost Jewish community of Ansbach.*

Opposite page, top: A close-up of the plaque that can be seen on the outer wall of the synagogue. Opposite page, bottom: A view of the synagogue's sanctuary

Hitler (top left) at a Nazi Party rally in Nüremberg, Germany, in 1928.

Hitler salutes a parade of SA troops in Nüremberg, Germany, in 1935.

Hitler Youth

Auschwitz

Adolf Hitler

Kristallnacht—*the infamous "Night of Broken Glass" of November 1938—left many Jewish homes ravaged.*

Soviet Foreign Minister Molotov (seated, right) signs the German-Soviet nonaggression pact in Moscow on August 23, 1939. German diplomat Joachim von Ribbentrop (standing, center) and Soviet Premier Joseph Stalin (second from right) stand behind him. Hitler later broke the pact, sending the Soviets to the side of the Allies.

Hitler poses triumphantly for a movie camera in Paris. With him are Nazi architect Albert Speer (left) and Nazi sculptor Arno Breker (right).

Ghetto inmates helped with the disembarking and the SS whipped us into a line. I could see the front of it already moving out toward the dirt road beyond the station before I was able to assemble those of the children around me who could walk and help the sick ones into a van. We walked for a half hour on that dusty road, saying very little. A young ghetto inmate, walking next to me, said at one point, "You can see the ghetto now!" I saw the steeple of a church and I noticed high walls, embankments, and a moat. It looked like a medieval fortress, this ghetto, and as we trudged over the bridge of the moat and through a wooden barrier in the side of the thick gate, I realized that that was exactly what it was. The young inmate, keeping step with me and the children, explained, "The place was built around 1790 by the Austrian Emperor Josef II as a garrison town for 6,000 soldiers and was named after the monarch's mother, Maria Theresa. We are about 60 kilometers (36 miles) from Prague. You will soon see the brick army barracks called Kasernen, the town square which was used as a parade grounds, the church, the city hall, and a number of houses, probably officers' quarters originally." Enclosing the whole colony were the walls and the embankments that I had seen from the road. I looked around, grateful for this unexpected geography lesson. I noticed an ominous stone complex outside the wall and was soon informed that this was a feared prison called *Kleine Festung* which was used for political prisoners. Modern Theresienstadt had been an ordinary Czechoslovakian town with a population of 5,000 until the German takeover of Czechoslovakia in March 1939. In December 1941, the Czech population was relocated to other towns and

Czech Jews were sent here. A few months later, coinciding with the Wannsee Conference of January 1942, Theresienstadt was officially declared a Jewish ghetto for 50,000 Jews from all of occupied Europe.

This was where fate had deposited me on this May day in 1943. I sat on my backpack in the courtyard of a barrack, waiting for the ghetto commandant to check me in, number me, and assign me a mattress and a soup can. This was where I would spend two precious years of my youth, although as I stood in the gloomy Kasernenhof, I didn't know that. When my turn to report to the SS finally came, I became # I/94-12709 and was assigned to a straw mattress on the top floor of the Hamburger Kaserne. Like all the other newcomers, I had to give up most of the belongings I had brought from Berlin. I had lost track of the children I had come with and of all the other people in my transport. I went to my new "home," fell onto the messy mattress and cried. For the first time in my life, in the midst of a dozen indifferent women, I was terribly alone.

For the next three weeks I cleaned the ghetto's children's home from eight in the morning until five o'clock, with time out to get in line for my noontime soup and bread. Then one lucky day I was sent to the home for new babies and their nursing mothers. From then on I worked in my profession again—in 12-hour shifts, seven to seven, either day shift or night. Except for long hours, hard work, very little (and very bad) food, and a bedbug- and lice-infested mattress, life in the ghetto seemed almost normal.

The ghetto appeared to be governed by Jews: Policemen, firemen, food personnel, all were Jewish. But everyone, from the Jewish ghetto governor and down, was under the merciless command of the Nazi camp commandant and his SS troops. If anything displeased them, the whole ghetto was punished. We could live with penalties such as no lights, little food, curfews, beatings and even executions. But the terror hanging over the ghetto, over every one of us, from the Jewish governor down to the little babies under our care, was the transports to the East.

Transports existed for two reasons: as a form of ghetto punishment and to thin the ghetto population. As Jews from nearly every country in Europe arrived in Theresienstadt and the ghetto population swelled beyond 50,000, inmates were collected for "labor transports" or "resettlement." This was the great deception. They were actually sent to Auschwitz to be gassed to death. Theresienstadt, the model ghetto created to show the world how humanely the Nazis treated Jews, was simply a way station for the Jews of Europe on the road to the killing centers in the East.

One day in June 1944, an SS order came to the ghetto government: Make the town and yourselves look respectable! An international commission would be visiting the ghetto within a month. We were given paints and brushes and ordered to work on houses along certain streets. Some Jews could get material to make drapes for their ground-floor windows only. Others received grass seed and rose bushes and were commanded to beautify the town square. We got better food rations and the young men who doled them out were suddenly wearing white cotton gloves. A children's playground sprang up, complete with sandboxes and swings. We were allowed—in fact ordered—to perform concerts in the town square and operas in designated localities. But while some Jews planted roses and rehearsed "The Bartered Bride" by the Czech composer Smetana for an official performance, other Jews were still being shipped out by the thousands to Auschwitz.

When the population was cut down and the ghetto ready to be inspected, a German preliminary review led by Adolf Eichmann drove through the prepared streets. Soon, on a pleasant July day, the International Commission, led by the Swedish Count Bernadotte along with Swiss and Danish representatives, drove through the same streets. They talked to a few adult Jews and to some children in the new playground. A few other young women and I marched by them, behind a hay wagon, rakes over our shoulders, out of the ghetto gates—and right back in again. I don't remember what songs we sang, but that was also part of the charade.

Was the Commission fooled into believing that this idealized place was a real concentration camp? And that all Nazi camps were like this? We did not know. We did not dare step out of our assigned roles for fear that our Nazi jailers would retaliate against the whole ghetto after the visitors left.

After the Swiss and Danes had left, the ideal ghetto was filmed: young men playing soccer in the barrack yard, women sitting in a coffeehouse drinking black coffee, old people strolling in the town square listening to music, and of course children hanging on the new swings and playing in the sandboxes. But it was a hoax.

Better food and superb music remained, but the Jewish administration was either transported out or sent to the Kleine Festung. Had something gone wrong? We never found out. Every one of us just hoped that we could hang on until the end of this awful war.

For me, the end of Theresienstadt came in February, 1945, when I heard that the next transport would go to Switzerland and that this one would take only 1,200 Jews. My friend Eva and I laughed. Oh sure, Switzerland. Just like that other time when a transport filled with children was going to Palestine but somehow never arrived there. But the rumors persisted. I had given up hope of ever seeing my mother and sister or any of my relatives again. Eva, too, was quite alone. So we took a chance and registered for the trip to Switzerland. We got numbers 1174 and 1175. I still have mine. We actually left the ghetto on February 4, 1945, with the war in Europe still raging, and 3 days later arrived at the railroad station in Constance, on the German-Swiss border. I tore off the yellow star I had been forced to wear for 4 years and stuffed it into my pocket. I looked out of the train window and for the first time in 12 years I saw people smiling.

I remained in Switzerland until the end of the war, located my father in New York, and was able to emigrate to the United States in April 1946. Years later I learned that 1,200 Jews were allowed to leave Germany as a result of negotiations between Heinrich Himmler, Hitler's powerful head of the SS, and the Swiss president Jean-Marie Musy. In exchange for the Jews, Himmler was given American dollars and the promise that he would receive favorable treatment at the hands of the victorious Allies. When Hitler found out about the arrangement, he forbade any further deals with the Allies and Himmler had to flee for his life.

My friend Eva and I and 1,198 other Jews from Theresienstadt were saved. Many years later, Eva's son married my daughter. The four grandchildren whom we share are a testimony to Jewish survival.

World Highlights, 1936-1940

Edward VIII becomes king of England. Gossip begins about his relationship with Mrs. Wallis Simpson. The Spanish Civil War begins. King Edward VIII of England abdicates and is succeeded by his brother, George VI. Trotsky is exiled from Russia. Chiang Kai-shek enters Canton. J. M. Keynes publishes The General Theory of Employment, Interest, and Money. *Hoover Dam is completed. Baseball Hall of Fame is founded at Cooperstown, N.Y. Insulin is used to control diabetes. Margaret Mitchell writes* Gone With the Wind. *Nylon stockings make their appearance. The film* Pygmalion *with Leslie Howard becomes popular, and the popular songs are "Bei mir bist Du schön" and "Whistle While You Work" and "Over the Rainbow." Benny Goodman's band brings new style to jazz music. Sigmund Freud dies in London. Igor Sikorsky builds the first helicopter. Madame Irène Curie-Joliot demonstrates the possibility of splitting the atom. Winston Churchill becomes prime minister of England.*

FINLAND

SWEDEN

Leningrad

ESTONIA

LATVIA

Riga ★

BALTIC SEA

LITHUANIA

RUSSIA

Kovino ★

EAST
PRUSSIA

Stutthof ▲

Danzig

Vilna ★

Grodno

Minsk

GERMANY

Treblinka

Baranowicze

Modlin ●

Bialystok ★

☆

Chelmno ☆ Warsaw ★

POLAND

Lódz' ★

Sobibor ☆

Brest-Litovsk

Gross-
Rosen ▲

Maidanek ☆

Auschwitz

Lublin ★

Babi Yar

Birkenau Belzec ☆

Szczebrzeszyn

Katowice ●

☆

Zwierzyniec

Kiev

Kraków ★

Lvov ★

CZECHOSLOVAKIA

Budapest ●

Jassy ■

HUNGARY

ROMANIA

	City
●	City
★	Ghetto
■	Transit Camp
▲	Concentration Camp
☆	Death Camp

Bucharest ●

BLACK SEA

CHAPTER 2

Events in Poland

Hitler was in power for six years before he embarked on open war. When he declared in his Reichstag speech of January 1939 that the German nation needed "an extension of living space in Europe," he had Poland in mind. Poland, Germany's neighbor to the east, was the largest state in Europe. Geographically, Poland linked Europe and Russia—the vast plain stretching from the Baltic Sea in the north to the Tatry and Carpathian Mountains in the south. Poland was blessed with rich soil, great mineral wealth and large coal deposits. The 30 million inhabitants included many ethnic minorities. A small number of Poles were titled landowners and many were farmers. Most Poles were Roman Catholic. Ten percent of the population was Jewish.

In 1934 Hitler drew up a 10-year peace treaty with Poland's Marshal Pilsudski so that he could increase his army undisturbed. Pilsudski had signed hoping the treaty would pacify the aggressive Fuehrer. Five years later, Hitler declared the treaty invalid. For him, a treaty was binding only as long as it served his purpose. The same year, 1939, he signed another treaty which served him for the next 22 months. This was a non-aggression pact with his old enemy, Soviet Premier Joseph Stalin. Hitler wanted to deal with Poland without having to fear Russian interference.

Hitler began his aggression against Poland by demanding the return to the Reich of the city of Danzig, or Gdansk, as it is known in Poland. It was a predominantly German city separated from the Reich by the Polish Corridor. In 1919, the Versailles Treaty had declared it an open city—meaning that as an undefended city, it could not be bombarded. But Hitler wanted it immediately, so that he could build highways across the Polish Corridor into East Prussia. Poland, backed by France and England, would not permit Germany access to Danzig nor to highways across her territory. The Allies gave their assurance that in the event of a war, France and England would come to Poland's aid. At this point, Hitler terminated the 1934 German-Polish agreement. He claimed Poland had subjected him to a policy of encirclement. In the summer of 1939, he increased the pressure regarding Danzig. But Poland, unlike the countries Hitler had intimidated in the recent past, stood firm.

In August, Hitler, as the supreme commander of the German Army, Navy and Air Force *(Luftwaffe)*, ordered the Army High Command to draw up Plan White, the invasion of Poland. On September 1, 1939, at 4:45 in the morning, one million German troops crossed the Polish frontier in Upper Silesia, East Prussia, and near Danzig. Simultaneously a fleet of Stuka bombers and Messerschmidts bombed the airfields and towns of Vilna, Grodno, Brest-Litovsk, Katowice, and Kraków, destroying most of the Poles' air power as it sat on the ground. Warsaw and

Modlin were attacked from the air at 9:00 AM. Poland suffered huge losses. The onslaught lasted three days. But Hitler had not yet declared war.

On September 3, France and England came to Poland's aid as they had promised and declared war on Germany. The American newspapers immediately called the conflict World War II.

On September 16, with most of Poland already in German hands, the siege of Warsaw began. The city endured incredible hardships, including widespread starvation and typhus. Bombs rained down mercilessly on the beautiful Polish capital. On the 27th, Warsaw surrendered. The Polish operation finished on October 6. The Germans took hundreds of thousands of Polish soldiers to Germany as prisoners.

Germany had introduced a new kind of war in Europe, a war of surprise attack delivered with spectacular speed. This was the *Blitzkrieg*—"lightning war."

Russian troops entered Poland on September 17 to help the Germans crush Poland. On the 28th, in accordance with a secret clause in their treaty, Hitler and Stalin divided Poland between them. The eastern part fell to Russia, the rest to Germany. For the next six years, the Poles lived under brutal foreign rule, their population ruthlessly destroyed. The leaders of the Polish government fled to Paris at the start of the German occupation and, after France fell the following year, moved to London and set up a Polish government-in-exile. From London, the Polish government organized and supported a Polish resistance and directed underground sabotage activities and freedom fighter movements against the hated occupiers.

In the German-occupied part of Poland, changes were felt immediately. On October 12, 1939, Heinrich Himmler, the powerful *Reichsfuehrer* of the SS, became Commissioner for the Consolidation of Occupied Poland; Hans Frank became Governor-General; Artur Seyss-Inquart, the Austrian Nazi who had helped bring about the annexation of Austria, became his deputy. Together, these men undertook the Germanization of Poland. Polish citizens were sent to work in Germany or to be slave labor in concentration camps. In either place they were marked for planned starvation. Their property was confiscated and given to ethnic Germans.

As for the 3.5 million Polish Jews, German planning called for their total annihilation. *Ostjuden*—Eastern Jews— had traditionally been the most pious, the most learned, most revered of all Jews in the eyes of world Jewry. The mystic Chasidic movement emerged in Poland. But it was also in Poland that the Jews had been persecuted most vigorously, by state, church, and the general population. Hostilities against Jews were first allowed in the 15th century and had frequently occurred ever since. When the Germans introduced anti-Semitic measures as early as October 1939, they found many willing allies among the locals.

Measures against the Polish Jews were carried out with utmost speed and followed the German model. Economic, social, and nutritional deprivation, physical and mental harassment, and visible ostracism by means of the yellow star or white armbands with Jewish stars on them were already familiar techniques. Added to the Polish solution of the Jewish question were the ominous ghettos.

On October 13, 1940, Hans Frank met with the head of

the Jewish Council of Warsaw, Adam Czerniakow, and informed him that a ghetto would be created in the inner city of Warsaw, around the Tlomakie Square Synagogue. The entire Jewish population of Warsaw was to be relocated within the ghetto's limits by the end of the month. Czerniakow was told to form a police force of 1,000 Jews to keep law and order among the Jews. A week later, on October 28, the *New Warsaw Courier* published the names of the streets which had been designated as the Jewish residential district, an area of roughly one-and-a-half square miles in the heart of the elegant city, a district of three- and four-story mansions with beautifully carved facades and wrought-iron balconies. By November 15, the Polish residents had moved out and the district was closed off from the surrounding city by the Red Wall, a high brick wall whose 10 gates were guarded by SS and their dogs. This ended all human movement between city and ghetto. For a while, streetcars continued their normal run through the district, passing through the area at top speed without stops. Until the route was changed, SS and Polish police in each carriage had to see that no one got off or on between gates. As the Jews of Warsaw were being pressed into the Jewish side behind the Red Wall, signs in German and Polish went up on the Polish side proclaiming it a quarantined area. All interchange between the two sides was strictly forbidden.

On March 17, 1941, Czerniakow was appointed Jewish Elder of the Warsaw Ghetto. His 24-man council was named the *Judenrat.* Jews could not use the terms fuehrer, leader, or any noun that implied authority. Jewish elders and Jewish councils everywhere were helpless, powerless, puppets of the Nazis. They were slaves who were ordered to carry out the destruction of the Jews in Europe, only to be destroyed themselves after the horrible job was done.

By now, the tree-lined streets and stately houses behind the Red Wall had become a prison for the 470,000 Jews of Warsaw, with thousands of refugees from surrounding towns and villages pouring in daily. By January 1941, the 170 rooms of 9 Stawki Street held 1,100 people. Not a single room was heated. The house had no running water and the toilets did not work. Dysentery and typhus broke out. Patients in rags remained in their rooms on narrow cots without blankets. The children suffered the most, dying in the streets. The stench of feces and death was unbearable. At 3 Dzika Street, 1,613 Jews lived in 153 rooms. At 9 Dzika Street, 8 rooms housed 136 people. Filth and hunger reigned. Every day the despair increased.

In November 1941, the Germans changed the size and the shape of the ghetto by tearing down the brick wall and building a new one. They made the ghetto smaller and divided it internally, building a footbridge from one part to the other. Food rations were cut down to one-third of those of the remaining Polish population. The ghetto's death toll reached 4,500 a month. People died on the crowded streets, their bodies covered by sheets of paper until a truck collected the many corpses for burial on the other side of the wall. There wasn't enough space in the ghetto for the living or the dead.

In July 1942, deportations began. Adam Czerniakow was ordered to have a daily quota of 5,000 Jews ready for "resettlement in the East" at the Umschlag Platz (a large assembly place). There they boarded the cattle cars and were transported to Treblinka, an extermination camp on the Bug River in Poland. On July 23, a few days after the quota order, Czerniakow was found dead, slumped over his desk. A note near his cold hand read:

> Three p.m. So far, 3,000 ready to go. By four p.m. according to orders, there must be 9,000. I am helpless. Sorrow and pity fill my heart. I cannot stand it any longer. My end will show every- body what must be done.

Janusz Korczak's Destiny

Janusz Korczak, the famous physician and benefactor of orphans, was born in Warsaw in 1878 or '79. At that time no one kept precise records. His given name was Hersh Goldszmit. While he was still a boy, his father be- came mentally ill and had to spend the rest of his life in a psychiatric institution. The burden of caring for his mother and younger siblings fell on Hersh's young shoul- ders. He soon became familiar with the hardship of being an orphan. He resolved to become a pediatrician. He also became a writer, exposing the deplorable conditions he found in orphanages to the world. Under the pen name Janusz Korczak, he wrote a series of articles and books explaining his ideas about modern orphanages and the status of children. The world listened and he was soon able to put his ideas to the test: He was appointed direc- tor of the Jewish Orphanage on Warsaw's Krochmalna Street. His reforms were duplicated in orphan homes in all of Poland and in other parts of the world.

In 1941, soon after the Warsaw Ghetto was established, Korczak was called to Gestapo headquarters and ordered to move the orphanage inside the ghetto walls. He was told that he and the home would henceforth be supervised by a German physician. Korczak and all his staff would have to take orders from him. Korczak was horrified. Move his 200 children from their bright three-story building on Krochmalna Street to cramped ghetto space? Have an SS man around day and night? How would his children adjust? Would his staff stay with him? Would Stefa Wilezynska, his friend and coworker, obey a German?

Korczak realized that if his children were to survive, he had to obey the Germans. As quickly as possible he resettled them behind the Red Wall. His loyal personnel stayed with him. Korczak determined to maintain the orphanage in as normal a way as possible despite the SS presence. On the streets of the ghetto and in every one of the overcrowded houses, dirt and filth was rampant, breeding sickness and death. Inside the orphanage, the first order was cleanliness. Every child helped with the daily task of cleaning. Despite the widespread hunger in the ghetto, the orphanage's cook was able to prepare enough food for the 200 children every day. Each morning, the persistent Korczak walked to the Jewish Community Office, where he asked wealthy ghetto inmates for food, clothing, and money for his children. The Jews in the ghetto soon had only rags to wear. But the children in the orphanage looked neat in the skirts, blouses, and shirts that Stefa and the housekeeper sewed for them. Classes continued in the established routine, plays were rehearsed, singing was encouraged. The children received lessons in ethics as well. When the older boys asked to join the underground resistance movement and begged for weapons to defend the home against the Nazis, Korczak and Stefa firmly refused, saying that violence could not be conquered by more violence. Instead, they tried to prepare the children for the time when they would have to appear at the Umschlag Platz for deportation.

The certainty of eventual deportation that hung over the whole ghetto hovered over the orphanage as well. Korczak's Polish friends tried to persuade him to save his life. They arranged for false papers and a hiding place outside the wall. Even the SS offered to let him go free if he agreed to tell the world lies about the conditions inside the ghetto and the nature of the transports. He refused. He would not leave his children in their greatest need. He would not stoop to the level of the Nazis.

The liquidation order came to the orphanage on August 4, 1942. The children were prepared. They dressed in their best outfits, and lined up in formation; 100 behind their beloved leader, 100 behind the equally beloved Stefa. Singing, they marched to the Umschlag Platz. Even there, the Nazi doctor who had supervised Korczak offered him safety once more. Korczak refused. The Nazi did not understand this man. Korczak, his two youngest charges in his arms, mounted the plank to the cattle car and gently urged the children forward. Stefa did the same at the next car. Just before the SS sealed the awful freight wagons, they both went inside, following the children to their destiny.

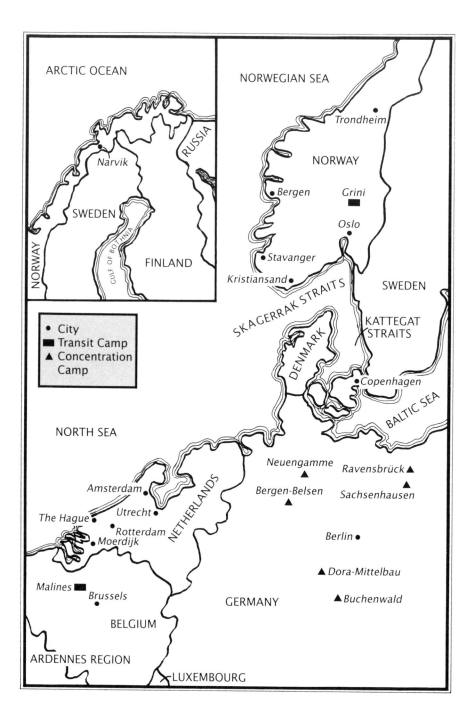

CHAPTER 3

The Occupation of Denmark and Norway

While Hitler devastated Poland in the east, six other countries declared their absolute neutrality: Sweden, Denmark, and Norway to the north; Holland, Belgium and Luxembourg to the west. Hitler promised publicly that he would honor their policy. Privately, he said that neutrality was meaningless and must be ignored. Of the six, only Sweden escaped invasion, perhaps because it did not lie directly in his path. Denmark and Norway were northern stepping-stones to England, as was Holland to his west. Belgium and Luxembourg were the route to France. He conquered these five countries in two swift operations only one month apart. Denmark and Norway were invaded on April 9, 1940, and Holland, Belgium and Luxembourg a month later, on May 10.

Denmark and Norway

Adjoining Germany at her northernmost tip and jutting out into the North Sea, Denmark was a monarchy with a population of 4 million people. Norway, lying across the Skagerrak Straits from Denmark, out in the Norwegian

Sea, was much larger but had fewer inhabitants. Norway's 3 million people had settled away from the mountainous interior, toward the fjords and the sea. They were an industrious fishing and seafaring nation with a history of shipbuilding. Both Denmark and Norway were monarchies. In fact, their two kings were brothers. In 1933 a Socialist party sprang up in Norway, the National Union Party of Vidkun Quisling. Quisling approached Hitler for his support of the movement and received it. Seven years later, when Hitler went into action against Norway, Quisling returned the favor and supported him.

The plan to conquer the two Scandinavian countries was code-named *Weserübung* (Weser Exercise), a plan to overpower and defeat Denmark and Norway in the quickest way possible. Denmark's airfields were to be used as a base for Hitler's invasion of Britain. Norway was needed to protect shipments of iron ore that came from Sweden down the coast of Norway to Germany. Hitler needed both Denmark and Norway if Germany's powerful navy was to sail into the North Atlantic.

General Nikolaus von Falkenhorst commanded Weserübung. On April 8, 1940, Falkenhorst ordered 7 German cruisers, 14 destroyers, and several torpedo boats out of the port of Bremerhaven and on to the North Sea, advancing north, but only at night. To fool the British, this fleet flew British flags and the crew answered calls for identification in English, giving the names of British ships. Early on the morning of Tuesday, April 9, these ships anchored at the Norwegian ports of Kristiansand, Stavanger, Trondheim, Bergen and Narvick. Ten thousand combat troops quickly made their way into the hearts of the cities. At the same time on that dark morning, 5,000 fully armed fighters parachuted from German planes into Oslo and Sola. When daylight came, Norway's major cities were full of German soldiers. They quickly linked up with Quisling's National Union Party.

Denmark was invaded and overrun simultaneously and in much the same way. At 8:30 in the morning, King Haakon VII in Oslo and King Christian X in Copenhagen, were handed identical ultimatums, each stating that the Germans had come not as conquerors but as guardians of the two countries' neutrality, protecting them from an imminent British takeover. The ultimatums requested the cooperation of each king and country and promised "no interference in governmental affairs either now or in the future." But should the requests be ignored or resistance encountered, there would be bloodshed and all loss of lives and damages would then be the responsibilities of the resisting kings.

Christian X capitulated at once. Perhaps because of the prompt surrender, or because Hitler liked the tall, blond, blue-eyed Danes, he made Denmark a model domain under German protection. King and cabinet remained in place and were not interfered with, at least not until 1942, when Hitler sent SS Chief of Security Werner Best to Copenhagen as *Reichskommissar* and SS *Standartenfuehrer* Rudolf Mildner as commissioner in charge of Jewish affairs. Once that happened, king and country, resenting the ever-tightening grip of the occupiers, organized one of the most effective resistance movements in all of occupied Europe. Germans found themselves hindered in every way, their orders ignored. When Best issued a decree to impose the wearing of the yellow star upon the Jews of Denmark, Christian X announced that if this were implemented, he and his family would be the first Danish citizens to wear this star as a badge of honor. "We have no Jews," he said publicly, "we have only Danes." The decree was not enforced. Denmark had 8,000 Jews— all very assimilated, respected, and protected by their king and government. Nevertheless, Hitler was fixated on eliminating all Jews, Danish Jews included.

When the German freighter *Wartheland* anchored at the Danish coast but failed to unload a cargo, rumors spread that the ship had come to take the Jews away. Those rumors were confirmed by the German officials. Yes, the roundups would begin October 1, 1943, and the Danes would be rid of their Jews a day later, a simple matter of two operations for the Gestapo. Then the Germans stole a list of the residences of Jewish citizens from official files. The Danish prime minister received secret word that the Jews were to be picked up at their homes, shipped to Germany, and on to Polish concentration camps. The prime minister threatened to resign if the Jews were harmed. Furthermore, his cabinet would resign, too. He also personally alerted leaders of the Jewish communities and the Danish Resistance. On city streets, Danes warned their Jewish friends; friends warned their neighbors and acquaintances; officials, both Jewish and Christian, made sure that the message of the Germans' plan was passed on. Strangers approached Jews and offered their homes and cottages for refuge, handing them keys; or gave them money, or just walked up to them with tears in their eyes and a warm word on their lips. Then, preparations for the evacuation to safety of the Jews of Denmark began. During the summer months of 1943, thousands of Jews were secretly shipped across the

Kattegat to Sweden and hundreds more were hidden in Danish homes. In October, when the Gestapo came with their stolen lists of Jews, they found very few Jews at home. Eventually, some 475 were rounded up and sent to Theresienstadt. But even there they remained under the protection of their government and were exempt from transports to death camps. In 1945, when the German occupation finally ended, all Jewish Danes returned home, travel expenses paid for by their monarchy.

The situation was very different in nearby Norway. Upon reading the German ultimatum on that April morning in 1940, King Haakon VII told his cabinet that he would fully understand if they decided to accept the German yoke in order to avoid spilling Norwegian blood. In such an event, however, he would be forced to abdicate. The ministers could not be less brave than their king and decided to resist. Haakon turned down Hitler's demands. Norway immediately organized a strong fighting force and asked for British naval aid. As Hitler had threatened, General von Falkenhorst met the resistance with a crushing assault. By utilizing the forces that had overrun Denmark and through continuous supplies of parachutists, he quickly built up the German strength to 80,000 troops. His ruthless fighting on the ground was supported by heavy air attacks aimed against Norwegian cities and the British naval forces that had come to help. The British fleet was forced back, and the king and his cabinet fled to London where they set up a government-in-exile. By June 10, just one month after the invasion, Norway surrendered in order to stop the bloodshed.

Norway had historically been one of the few refuges of peace for European Jews, but with the German invasion,

peace for Norwegian Jews ended abruptly. Hitler put SS
Kommissar Josef Terboven in charge of the Jewish question in Norway. Terboven received and accepted the full
cooperation of Quisling and his party. Anti-Jewish actions
began at once. In May the beautiful Trondheim synagogue was smashed to pieces, a swastika placed where
the Star of David had been. Holy objects were demolished and eternal lamps were used for German target
practice. Radios were confiscated; travel was restricted;
trips abroad forbidden altogether. Soon the Germans demanded membership lists from all Jewish communities,
the first step toward their disintegration. At first, only
refugees from other parts of Europe were arrested, taken
to the Norwegian concentration camp at Grini. The Jewish community was agitated but not alarmed. In June
1941, Jewish property and real estate were confiscated.
Jews living in northern Norway were arrested and sent to
forced labor camps in the Arctic. Jews living in central
Norway were declared illegal aliens. Many fled to Sweden but many others remained. Events were fast approaching a state of alarm for the Jews of Norway.

In September 1941, a Norwegian policeman was shot
by a group of young Jews who were trying to escape to
Sweden. Quisling ordered the roundups to begin. "Europe is overrun by Jews like grasshoppers!" he declared,
and it was time that Norway dealt with its Jewish problem. Mass deportations followed. Jews were loaded into
the troopship *Donau* and shipped to German ports. From
there they were transported by train to their deaths at
Auschwitz. With the exception of one letter of protest
from a group of Norwegian bishops and professors, the
citizens of Norway voiced no objections.

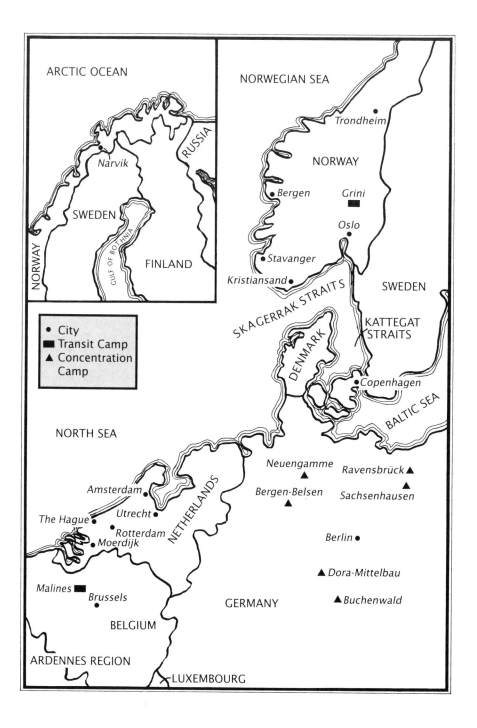

ARCTIC OCEAN

RUSSIA

Narvik

SWEDEN

GULF OF BOTHNIA

FINLAND

NORWAY

NORWEGIAN SEA

Trondheim

NORWAY

Bergen

Grini

Oslo

Stavanger

Kristiansand

SKAGERRAK STRAITS

SWEDEN

KATTEGAT STRAITS

DENMARK

Copenhagen

BALTIC SEA

• City
■ Transit Camp
▲ Concentration Camp

NORTH SEA

Neuengamme

Ravensbrück ▲

Bergen-Belsen

Sachsenhausen ▲

Amsterdam

NETHERLANDS

Utrecht

The Hague

Rotterdam

Moerdijk

Berlin •

▲ Dora-Mittelbau

Malines ■

Brussels

GERMANY

▲ Buchenwald

BELGIUM

ARDENNES REGION

LUXEMBOURG

CHAPTER 4

The Invasion of Holland, Belgium, and Luxembourg

While Hitler's soldiers were plunging from the skies over Norway in April 1940, he was giving orders to begin Plan Yellow, the invasion of neutral Holland, Belgium, and Luxembourg. His ruthless Blitzkrieg had proven successful. He had extended his nation's living space toward the north and had assured food supplies and war materials by bringing two more countries under his command. Now he resolved to occupy Holland to the west of the Reich for the same reasons he had occupied Denmark—as a stepping-stone to England. He wanted Belgium because he planned to invade France across the unfortified Franco-Belgian border—not through the Maginot Line that France had built to protect itself. The small duchy of Luxembourg would be overrun simply because it lay between Germany, Belgium and France. He meant to attack Luxembourg, Belgium and Holland all on the same day.

The monarchy of Holland had always considered itself invasion-proof, protected by an elaborate system of Dutch dikes, canals and artificial waterways that criss-crossed the flat land. The green, tulip-dotted countryside had

almost no natural obstacles besides those waterways to
protect its dairy farms and lovely cities. In 1940 Holland
had a population of 13 million people who wanted nothing more than to be left in peace. But this was not their
fate. Holland was overpowered in five days. During the
subsequent five years of bondage, it suffered the most
hardship and famine of all the occupied countries in
western Europe. Hitler ordered three army groups into
the campaign. One was to drive through the Ardennes
Forest into Belgium with 42 divisions; a second would
march into Holland across the Ruhr region with 30 divisions; the third would take the southern route through
Luxembourg into Belgium with 19 divisions. The onslaught struck the unsuspecting West at precisely 4:10
AM on May 10, 1940. Later that morning the familiar ultimatums were delivered to Queen Wilhelmina of Holland, King Leopold of Belgium and Grand Duchess
Charlotte of Luxembourg. This time, Hitler's lies included "protecting" the stricken countries not only from
a British invasion but from an imminent French conquest
as well.

Again, everything went according to Hitler's plans. On
May 10, the Grand Duchess quickly accepted the ultimatum and escaped across the border to France while her
cabinet fled to London. Her tiny country was taken over
by SS Kommissar Gustav Simon who immediately sent
most of its 300,000 inhabitants to German labor camps
and wiped out its ancient Jewish community of 4,000
people.

In the Netherlands, while Queen Wilhelmina was reading the German declaration on that fateful Friday morning,
German Stukas divebombed The Hague, Rotterdam, and

Moerdijk, devastating those beautiful cities. Dutch General Winkelmann's forces tried to defend the country but were unable to halt the bombing or stem the invasion, even with help from the Allies. Loss of life and damage to the Dutch cities was so great that Winkelmann asked for an armistice on the 15th, and Holland capitulated. An underground movement, supported by Queen Wilhelmina and her government-in-exile in London acted immediately, harassing and sabotaging the captors and, later, saving the lives of many Jews.

Holland had a Jewish population of about 140,000, one of the oldest Jewish communities in Europe. Jews had enjoyed Dutch citizenship since the Middle Ages and had taken an active part in the affairs of government there since 1797. They had settled almost exclusively in the three major cities—Amsterdam, Rotterdam and The Hague. When anti-Jewish measures began, this natural concentration aided the Germans in collecting their victims and sending them to their deaths. Few were able to escape since the country offered no pastoral hiding places, no thick forests or remote mountains, and no neutral borders nearby. Safety could be found only in the attics and hidden back rooms of sympathetic Dutch Gentiles. At the start of the occupation, the Austrian SS officer Artur Seyss-Inquart was recalled from his post in occupied Poland and appointed Reichskommissar for occupied Holland. Another feared Austrian, Hans Albin Rauter, was made his deputy. Willi Zopf and Ferdinand Aus der Fünten were chosen to deal with the Jewish question. One hundred twenty thousand Jews were deported to concentration camps. Only 15,000 survived. Hundreds of thousands of Dutch citizens were deported to labor camps in

Germany; thousands more had been mercilessly killed by the invaders. Even after the Allies landed on the beaches of Normandy on June 6, 1944, Holland would be caught in a pocket of German resistance. Another year would pass before the stricken land was finally free.

Leesha's Resistance

In the Bornstein house in The Hague, Friday was normally spent in joyous preparation for the Sabbath. But May 10, 1940, was far from a normal Friday. Before sunrise, Father, Mother, 17-year-old Hava, 15-year-old Paul, and 4-year-old Jackie were roused from sleep by the German assault on Holland. Within days their beloved homeland was in German hands. What would happen to it? To the Dutch citizens? And how would the occupiers treat the Dutch Jews? During the next weeks and months, Jewish friends and neighbors attempted to smuggle themselves into Switzerland, emigrate to Palestine, or register for quota numbers to get into the United States. But the Bornstein family had nowhere to go. Some Jews went underground, getting false papers and living illegally with kind Gentiles. One couple of the Bornsteins' acquaintance committed suicide. The family pondered the future. No possibilities presented themselves, no doors seemed to open for them. Hava begged her parents to let her join a group of pioneers who were emigrating to Palestine, but her parents would not allow their young daughter to leave without them. Before long, Dutch schools and universities would no longer admit Jewish students and Hava had to abandon her dream of studying medicine. But she wanted desperately to do something. When she heard that hospitals were looking for student nurses, she applied immediately and to her joy was admitted at Joodse Invalide Hospital in Amsterdam. She embraced her family in farewell. She didn't know that her beloved father would soon be sent to the dreaded Dutch concentration camp Westerbork and from there to Auschwitz to be murdered in the gas chambers. Her mother and little brother would be caught in a street roundup in The Hague and also sent to Auschwitz, where they were gassed on arrival. Her brother Paul, who had gone into hiding, would be denounced and sent to Sobibor to be killed there.

To control her despair, Hava let work and study engulf her and devoted herself to her patients. Then one day in February 1943, the order came to liquidate the Joodse Invalide Hospital the very next day. All day long, Hava helped the old and the sick, the blind and the senile into the SS vans, knowing in her heart that these people were going to their deaths, and that she had to go with them. She was about to step into the gloomy truck when a forceful will to live claimed her, filling her with a boldness she didn't know she possessed. She hid her white uniform with the yellow star under her coat and calmly walked past the van, past the SS guards, the police, out into the traffic of Sarfatistraat. She went to the other Jewish hospital, the Netherland Israelite Hospital at Nieuwe Keizersgracht. She was assigned to the male ward.

One day she was told to bring medication to a "special" patient, a man under police guard. When she stepped into the room she saw a young man, obviously very ill, gazing at her intently and she understood in a flash of insight that this man wanted to tell her something. She bent over him, pretending to give him medication, and listened carefully to his low voice. Somehow she knew that whatever he was going to tell her would have to be memorized. He whispered an address and said, "The password is 'The tulips are red!'" This had to be a contact with the secret Underground Resistance movement! She resolved to find the address and use the password on her next free day.

The house she was sent to was ordinary. The password worked and inside she found a room full of people who introduced themselves with apparently assumed names. They seemed to know her. Had her bold escape from the Joodse Invalide become known to the Underground? The group informed her that they were indeed members of the Underground movement and that one of their tasks was to hide Jews with Dutch Gentile families. Her patient had been assigned to provide false papers and food stamps for the hidden Jews when he was caught by the Germans. Now they wanted her to continue his activities. As a first step they asked her to be their link to the hospital, to watch for patients who wanted to go into hiding or mothers desperate to save their newborn babies. She left her new friends with a feeling of mission and elation.

Back at the hospital, she found a pretense to enter the special patient's room. With her eyes she sent a silent message telling him that she was involved. She could see the relief in his face.

SS orders came for evacuation of this hospital. Again, Hava helped unhappy people into those terrible vans and this time she stepped into the last one, backpack in hand, ready to share her patients' fate. The vans drove directly to the railroad station and up the planks which led to the waiting cattle cars. Inside the cars, Hava walked among the sick, giving assurance that she did not really feel.

Il Duce—*Italy's Benito Mussolini (seated, left) attends a rally with Hitler in Munich, Germany, in 1940.*

Hungarian Jews are rounded up and deported in cattle cars to concentration camps.

More than one and a half million people were killed in Auschwitz (left), a Nazi concentration camp in southern Poland.

*1943: President Roosevelt (foreground) and British Prime Minister
Winston Churchill meet to discuss war strategy in Morocco.*

Above: The Nazis forced more than 500,000 Jews to live in the Warsaw ghetto. Below: In 1943, after crushing a ghetto uprising, the Nazis burned the entire ghetto—killing the Jews who had not yet been transported to the death camps.

British Prime Minister Winston Churchill (second from left) and members of his staff examine the damage done by German bombs in London.

Medics help a wounded soldier in France, 1944.

German storm troopers surrender to the U.S. 100th Infantry Battalion in Italy, July 1944.

U.S. infantrymen stop for a meal on their way to La Roche, Belgium, in early 1945.

April 1945: As the Germans near defeat, U.S. soldiers run through the smoke-filled streets of St. Wernberg, Germany.

These survivors of a Nazi concentration camp at Eversee, Austria, were liberated by U.S. soldiers in May 1945.

The end of the war: Before Allied witnesses, Alfred Jodl (center, holding pen) signs Germany's surrender papers on May 7, 1945. The following day, Hitler's successor, Alfred Doenitz, officially surrendered.

Survivors of the concentration camp Lager Nordhausen

These women, crowded into a concentration camp barrack (left),
and chopping wood (above), have been liberated by Allied soldiers.

Prisoners of Dachau concentration camp in Germany celebrate their liberation at the end of the war.

German Jewish refugees arrive in the United States.

Outside, an SS man walked up and down the long train calling: "Brother de Leeuw! Lilly Bromet!"

Hava was electrified. Were these two people to be pulled out of the transport? And they couldn't be found? Instinctively, she grabbed her backpack and jumped to the platform. She stepped firmly before the SS man and said: "I am Lilly Bromet," praying in her heart that he would not ask for identification. He looked at her coldly and told her to go back to work at the hospital. Behind her, the freight train began to move.

In July, just a month later, the vans came again. This time they stopped at the Hollandse Schouwburg, a collection center in the city of Amsterdam, where the Jews had to wait until freight trains were available. On the fifth day of the unbearable wait a young man approached her casually. When he had made sure no one was close enough to hear, he said quietly that she had been chosen for rescue by the Underground. He told her to be in the attic of the Schouwburg the next morning at 6:00 AM and from there to follow orders carefully.

The Underground hid Hava in the old Joodse Invalide while they prepared false identity papers for her. When they finally came, she was Elisabeth Bos, a Dutch Gentile. Her code name was Leesha.

For a short while, Leesha was placed in a convalescent home in a suburb of Haarlem. There, using her nurse's activities as a cover, she received orders from the Underground and carried them out evenings and on her days off. One day a contact man came and took her with him to Leiden. The person who had cared for the hidden Jews had been caught, and Leesha was to take over his responsibilities. This was a formidable task, for there were 180 or more hidden Jews. Leesha's duty was to provide them with food stamps, false papers, money, news, and encouragement. She was given a bicycle and an address where she could find a room and then she was on her own.

The war dragged on. The Germans confiscated all Dutch goods, all produce, every farm animal they could lay their hands on, and planned to send their loot to Germany. Dutch railroad workers, enraged by this plunder and encouraged by their government-in-exile, went on a nationwide strike. The Germans threatened terrible revenge on the strikers and their families. The Underground helped hide these patriots and again Leesha was able to play a role. Through one of her friends, she became a member of yet another arm of the Resistance movement, the *Strijdent Nederland*.

Holland suffered terribly. People ate tulip bulbs to keep from starving and cut down park trees for firewood. Leesha lay awake nights praying that the Allies would come in time to save her country. On April 29, 1945, they did. The roar that Leesha heard that day was the sound of deliverance: Four hundred fifty British bombers flew low over Amsterdam and dropped thousands of tons of food. The next day, American bombers did the same over all of Holland. The hunger was over. The war would be over soon and she had survived it. But Leesha found that she had survived it alone.

In 1947, she married one of the liberators, the Canadian Captain Dr. Isaac B. Rose. With him she started a new life in Canada. They now live in Israel.

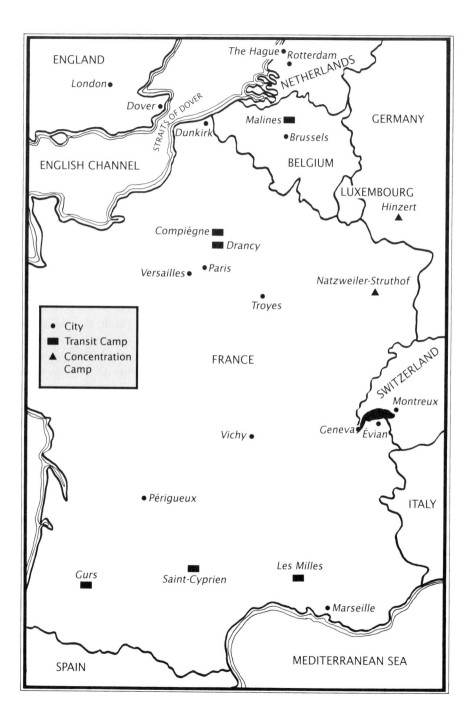

The Germans in Belgium

Holland's neighbor to the south, the kingdom of Belgium, was an equally lovely, cultured, and industrious land with rolling lowlands and picturesque cities. Belgium had a population of 10 million people. Belgium resisted the German terror for 18 days before it, too, surrendered. When Nazi tanks came crashing through the Ardennes Forest on May 10, 1940, and German bombers unleashed airborne death over cities and airfields, King Leopold III was ready to surrender to the Germans at once. But his cabinet insisted on resisting and with Allied help, the Belgians fought heroically against insurmountable odds.

Two weeks later, after Belgium had taken a terrible beating by the Germans, the ministers advised King Leopold III to flee to London. But the young king stubbornly insisted on staying, even at the risk of falling into enemy hands. His government fled without him and set up an exile government which guided Belgian resistance from London. Antwerp fell to the Germans on May 18. Ten days and much bloodshed later, on May 28, Leopold surrendered to the invaders and was eventually taken to

Germany as a prisoner. His country came under the military command of General Alexander von Falkenhausen.

The Belgian community of 65,000 Jews fared better under the military commander than her neighbors did under the customary SS commissars. Unlike the SS chiefs, German generals did not see the destruction of the Jews in their territory as their primary task. A country considered itself fortunate to get a military officer as the highest occupational ruler instead of an SS Kommissar, but such luck was rare.

In Belgium, General Falkenhausen permitted and even encouraged thousands of Jews to cross the frontiers into France before he embarked on the prescribed anti-Semitic procedures. He postponed the roundups as long as he could. When at last he did allow mass transportations to take place in June 1942, he declared Belgian Jews exempt from deportation. He restricted arrests to the many thousands of Jews who had come to Belgium as refugees from all the other occupied countries in Europe. But even among those unhappy people, many found protection and hiding places with the anti-German Belgians.

In the spring of 1945, the Germans were driven out of Belgium and the king's cabinet returned. King Leopold III, who had been liberated from German imprisonment and was living in Switzerland, was invited back home in 1950. Thousands of Belgians had perished during the bloody war and grim occupation.

Twenty-five thousand Jews of the original 65,000 were still in the country. Of those who were sent to concentration camps, a few survivors returned to Belgium, among them Eliezer Flinker, a survivor of Auschwitz. Alone, old and broken from his ordeal, he searched out the house on the outskirts of Brussels where he, his wife, and their seven children had been in hiding for nearly two years. Nothing was there for him but sad memories—and a diary. His son Moshe, killed in Auschwitz at age 16, had left a written record.

Moshe's Fate

Moshe Flinker was born in Holland in 1926 into a large, deeply religious family. His father, Eliezer, a wealthy businessman, conducted some of his business in Brussels. He crossed the border to Belgium regularly every week. In November 1942, with the persecution of the Jews in Holland in full force, Moshe could hear his parents discussing the future. Should they flee to Switzerland as many of their friends had done? Unfortunately, some of them had been caught and sent back for deportation. With his solid connections in Brussels, the elder Flinker convinced his wife that Belgium should be their destination, explaining to her and Moshe that Jews were somewhat safer under German military governance in Belgium than under Nazi rule in Holland. Moshe couldn't see much difference in the two types of German occupation but when his father arranged for the large family to cross illegally into the neighboring country, he felt relieved. At least the endless discussions about the future would stop.

By means of large bribes, Mr. Flinker was able to register his family as Dutch citizens living in Brussels, and with the help of his business contacts he found a house. They were safe for the moment. But they needed to keep out of sight. Neighbors might become suspicious of a new family with seven children. There was always the fear that a neighbor might denounce them to the Germans.

Moshe's initial feeling of safety soon gave way to new emotions. He was bored. He worried. He doubted his God. Because he had no one to talk to, he started a diary. The first entry was dated November 24, 1942, the last, April 7, 1944.

Those 17 months in hiding were months of boredom for the boy. Going to school was out of the question and being seen outdoors during school hours was dangerous. Having no friends, he stayed indoors even after school hours. He never dared venture to the park or to a library. For a while, he tried to teach French to his sister. When this didn't work, he tried to learn Arabic. But his mind was so filled with worries that he soon gave up such projects. His diary was his friend and recording his anxieties became his only activity.

Moshe knew that his father had to cash in large portions of stocks to pay for their residents' permits, black market food coupons, and clothes for all of them. "Bribing and begging from month to month, is that the way You want us to live, God?" Moshe asked his diary. "Do You want us to be shut in, fearing every knock at the door? Do You really want me to have nothing to do but pray and worry? God? Is this Your will?"

In December 1942, the family celebrated Hanukkah— the Jewish Festival of Lights—in hiding. Moshe begged the Lord for a miracle. "Send me a sign, oh God, something, so that I will know that You don't mean to destroy Your people! Oh Lord, perhaps You will send the Messiah while I am lighting these Hanukkah candles!" Moshe sang the "Maoz Tzur" with fervor: "Rock of Ages, come to our aid! Hear my prayers! If they are unworthy, answer the prayers of saintly men!"

No miracle occurred. On the contrary, Moshe had only bad news to record in his diary. He heard that one of his friends had been killed while trying to cross the border from Holland to Belgium just as he himself had done only a month earlier. Was the friend betrayed? More bad news: Another friend was turned back at the Swiss border with his whole family. "Do the nations know that we are being deported for slave labor by the thousands every day?" he wrote. "Will no country help us?"

And one day father brought home the most shocking news of all. The deported Jews were not used for labor—they were being killed. And, father continued, other nations probably knew of the massacres, yet did nothing to stop them. Pain engulfed the boy. He wished he could die rather than hear such horrible things. His people being killed? Jews like himself murdered? Where could he look for consolation? In the Bible? The Prophets? He took up the Book of Lamentations and said the dirges: "Return us, oh Lord, unto Thee and we shall return."

In January 1943, Moshe heard of the fighting in Russia, that the German armies were retreating. He took this as the sign from God for which he had waited all these many lonely months. "You did hear my prayers, Ruler of the Universe! You will not forsake us! You will beat the Germans in Russia and set the Jews free." Still all around him Jews were picked up, either on the streets or in their houses to be sent to their doom. Moshe prayed for them from the very depth of his heart, morning, noon and night.

The winter of 1943 was unusually severe in Brussels and the Flinkers were cold and hungry. They had nothing to do but sit in the apartment. Emptiness was in Moshe's heart. "Why, Lord of the Universe," he wrote in his diary, "do You let Your people experience such anguish? Such suffering will not bring the Jews back to You! On the contrary, they will think there is no God at all in Heaven."

He yearned to go to Palestine to make it a homeland for all Jews. Again he tried to study Arabic. Perhaps he could become a diplomat in this Jewish homeland of his dreams, helping make peace between Jews and Arabs. He thought of the many times in history that his people had endured persecution. Was there a difference in persecution throughout the ages? Again, he wrote onto the cold pages of his diary: "Why do You allow this, oh Lord!" He delved into the *Zohar*, the mythical book of Jewish learning, and thought he had found an answer: "We were expelled from our land because of our sins," he wrote. "Now we must first repent completely. We must be cleansed by suffering before the Lord will let us return." As he stood before his God in daily prayer, he asked fervently that God let His people live and reach their homeland, Palestine.

Winter flowed into spring and Moshe kept writing in his diary, asking the disturbing question: "Why!" He kept saying his daily prayers, wondering if they were heard. He was very depressed. But he never lost faith in God and in God's mercy.

Spring became summer. Moshe fasted on Tisho b'Av, commemorating the destruction of the First Temple in Jerusalem, 2,529 years earlier. He wept both for the destroyed Temple and for the suffering of his people in Europe. He prayed for the Messiah to come to lead all the Jews out of slavery to safety. He realized with a start that there were only three countries left in continental Europe that were free of Hitler's influence, three countries in which the Jews did not have to fear for their lives: Sweden, Portugal and Switzerland.

During that fall and into the winter of 1944, Moshe rarely wrote in his diary. What was there to write about? God had apparently not heard him, was not answering him, had sent no sign to him. God was silent. Moshe no longer dreamed of safety or of becoming a diplomat. He had stopped studying, stopped trying to find consolation or even answers, stopped reading the Bible and the Zohar.

In April 1944, the Flinker family made preparations to observe Passover, the holiday of liberation, in a climate of doom. Father had been able to get some matzo—the special unleavened Passover bread, and even a chicken, a rare treat. As Moshe's mother salted and koshered the chicken and Moshe helped set the Seder table for the evening celebration, Gestapo agents stormed into the apartment. The whole family was taken away and sent to Auschwitz. Eliezer Flinker and two of his daughters were the family's only survivors.

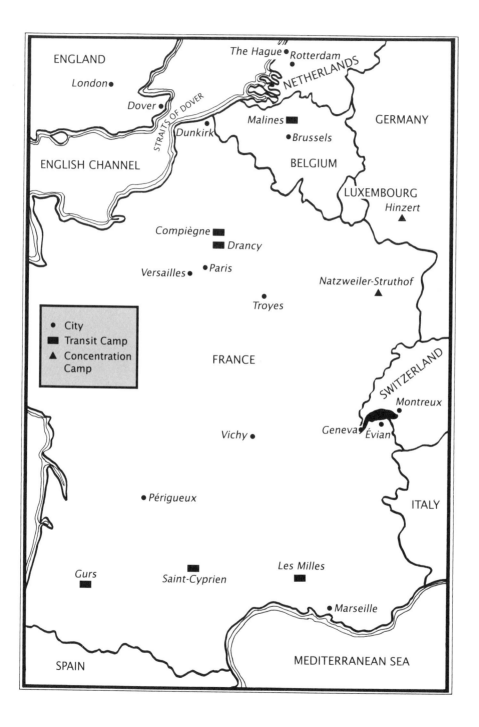

CHAPTER 6

France Falls

Hitler considered France Germany's irreconcilable and mortal enemy. Along with England, France was the country he most wanted to conquer and humiliate. After Germany's surrender to the Allies at the end of World War I, the conditions of surrender were drawn up in France, at the Palace of Versailles. At Compiègne, in France, defeated Germany was forced to accept the degrading conditions of the Versailles Treaty. The Treaty imposed political, military, and economic submission on Germany, granted autonomy to former German areas, and demilitarized the Rhineland, ending the German Empire, the Second Reich of Kaiser Wilhelm II.

Hitler, when creating the Third Reich in 1933, used the Versailles Treaty as a vehicle of propaganda. He claimed world Jewry had drawn up this shameful document. The Treaty restricted his nation, and he declared it invalid. By the time his armed and armored divisions stood before the borders of France in June of 1940, the Treaty lay broken behind him: Germany was fully armed and all the regions and countries that had been taken from Germany in 1919 were again part of the Reich. Twenty-one years after the Treaty was signed, Hitler had brought back into the Reich the Saar region, Austria, the Czech-Slovak state, Memel on the Baltic Sea and the Free City of Danzig. The Rhineland on the border of France was fully militarized and Hitler was ready to take his revenge—ready to take France. Hitler asserted that the Jews were solely responsible for Germany's defeat in World War I and for the humiliating provisions of the Treaty. This was why he was punishing the Jews. Now he was out to get France.

In France, tolerance was practiced: Race was not recorded on French birth certificates. The 40 million French tried to feel secure and protected from German attack behind their Maginot Line, a chain of fortresslike military installations, which stretched from Luxembourg to Switzerland along the German-French border. On May 19, 1940, General Maxime Weygand took command of the French Army, not dreaming that only a month and a few days later he would be signing the French surrender in the very Compiègne forest where Germany had been brought to her knees in 1919. While the German band played the German national anthem, "Deutschland Über Alles," Weygand signed France away to Hitler. Hitler coveted France's iron and wheat; its great art—the Cezannes and Manets and Renoirs. He needed strong young Frenchmen for slave labor. For the moment, Germany was on top of the world.

While General Bock was still waiting for Belgium to surrender to him, the armies of the German Generals Küchler, Kleist, Kluge and Guderian pressed toward the West, toward the British and French troops who had come to Belgium's aid. But on May 24, just as Guderian's and

Kleist's Panzer corps advanced on Calais and Dunkirk and were nearly in reach of the Dover Straits and the English Channel, an order to halt came from Hitler. This illogical command enabled the British, French, and some Belgian troops to evacuate the threatened area and to reassemble at the French border. When Hitler lifted the order two days later and the Germans could advance once more, plans had been made to get most of the Allied forces safely out of the Nazi's reach. The "miracle of Dunkirk" occurred in which a third of a million men were carried to safety across the English channel in anything that floated. This was Hitler's first great mistake. One day these men would fight again. For the time being, however, the Allies were broken. On May 28, 1940, Belgium surrendered and by May 30 the Allies were preparing to defend France.

German morale was high from victories of the previous month. French morale was low. Not even British Prime Minister Churchill's radio messages to his French allies could give them a boost. Nor could his public and private support of French Premier Paul Reynaud stave off the demands in Reynaud's cabinet for surrender.

Reynaud had formed a new French cabinet only three months before. In May, he appointed the aging Marshal Henri Pétain to be his vice premier. From the very beginning, Pétain wanted to surrender to Germany, believing that then the fighting in Europe would stop and France would receive favorable cease-fire terms as a reward for her submission. Reynaud, on the other hand, proposed moving the French government to North Africa (where France had colonies) and together with England continue fighting until Hitler was defeated. Heavy bombing and advancing German armies did force the government to move on June 11, 1940. They fled first to Tours and then to Bordeaux where Reynaud resigned under pressure from Pétain's followers.

On June 17, Pétain took over the government and formed a new cabinet with Pierre Laval. Laval agreed with Pétain's defeatist philosophy. Indeed, he had admired Hitler ever since 1933 and now looked forward to welcoming him personally to Paris. Together Pétain and Laval resolved to surrender at once. Their request for a truce reached Hitler at his war headquarters in Sedan at the French border on June 17, but he made the French wait until he conferred with his friend and ally, the Italian *Duce*, Mussolini.

Mussolini had entered the war on Hitler's side only a few weeks before. He had hoped to get a part of France or at least some French colonies in North Africa for his efforts. But Hitler had other plans. Instead of carving France up, he schemed to divide the country against itself: He would occupy the northern part; Pétain and Laval would govern the south with headquarters in Vichy. In this way he hoped to weaken France and prevent an uprising.

On June 22, 1940, only 17 days after he had first attacked France, Hitler presented Weygand with the conditions of surrender in the forest of Compiègne, on the very spot of Germany's humiliation in 1919. The same railroad car where once France had dictated terms to Germany was dragged from a museum and erected again on now-rusty rails. With Field Marshal Hermann Goering at his side and the German High Command behind him, Hitler marched onto the historic spot, his face ablaze with triumph. This time he did the dictating. France was divided, all German prisoners of war were to be released, and the French would pay the entire cost of the occupation. Hitler kept the one million French prisoners of war that he had taken in the month of fighting and used them for forced labor. In time, he would ship another million French citizens to the Reich's labor camps. He shipped France's raw materials and food to Germany. He also emptied France's wonderful museums. With the band playing German victory marches, Weygand signed the harsh document. The railroad car was immediately dismantled and triumphantly shipped to Berlin. The memorial park in the forest of Compiègne was demolished.

While the swastika was raised over Paris and French citizens wept, Hitler, with columns of SS troops, strode through Paris. Napoleon's Tomb, the Arc de Triomphe, the Tuileries, the Eiffel Tower—all his! A German government was set up in Paris. Two German generals, Otto von Stülpnagel and Karl Heinrich von Stülpnagel, took over the military administration of northern France. SS Chief Adolf Eichmann took upon himself the Solution of the Jewish Question in France.

The Jewish population of France could trace its origins back to the 6th century and the movement of the Jews out of the Roman Empire. By the 10th century, French Jewry was already well established and had produced eminent rabbis and scholars, the most famous of them Rashi of Troyes. In 1791 French Jews were granted individual rights and the great Emancipation began. It spread from France to neighboring countries and, by the beginning of the 19th century, to all of Europe. Ghetto walls came down and assimilation took place. Jews settled in all of France as respected citizens. At the time of the surrender to Hitler, France had an estimated Jewish population of 300,000—estimated because France had never made a distinction between Jews and non-Jews in statistics.

Immediately after the conquest of Paris, the Nazis began the persecution of French Jews and all other Jews who had fled there from already occupied countries. The Nazis also sought to capture anyone who opposed the German occupation, either openly or by aiding the French Resistance. French citizens were sent to the Reich for slave labor. French prison complexes in and near Paris became collection centers of the French Jews who from there were sent to German extermination centers.

Fania's Survival

Fania Fenelon was a beautiful and spirited young French musician. Because she was only half Jewish, she had not been deported at once and had managed to continue her career as a cabaret singer in Paris even though the Germans controlled France. But she hated singing for the Germans and secretly worked with the French Resistance, helping them every chance she had. And then, someone denounced her to the German police. One morning in the fall of 1943, as she arrived home from work, she found the Gestapo waiting for her. She was taken to Drancy Prison in Paris and from there, on a cold January morning in 1944, sent on a 50-hour journey in a dark, crowded, unventilated cattle car. When the doors finally opened, the glare of searchlights revealed watch towers, barbed wire fences, and a red night sky. Where was she? Who were those skeletal, empty-eyed robots in striped prison pajamas? Where were the trucks with painted red crosses taking the old people, the women and children? Fania, wrapped in her fur coat and glad for some air, refused a ride into the camp on the trucks and walked arm in arm with her friend Clara. It took them a half-hour to reach the gate that proclaimed Work Camp. To their horror they had arrived at Birkenau, the extermination camp of Auschwitz.

They were herded into a huge amphitheater and stripped of all their belongings: the fur coat went first, then the boots, handbags, jewelry; then all their clothing until the two young women stood naked. Next, their hair was shaved off. Crowding women pushed them along, made them step over the mass of coiling hair that quickly accumulated around their feet. Then they were tattooed. Number 74862 was branded indelibly into Fania's forearm. Someone handed her a pair of men's boots, a striped prison uniform with a yellow triangle sewn onto it and a kerchief. She was ordered into line alongside Clara and marched to bunker 25.

A mean-looking woman gave orders, rushing them along. As Fania struggled to keep pace in her men's boots, she learned that this woman was a *kapo*—short for the Jewish camp police, and that bunker 25 was the quarantine block. She dared to ask the kapo what had become of the people from her transport, the ones who rode into camp on those red cross trucks. The kapo pointed to tall chimneys 50 yards away and said without any emotion that those people were going up in smoke over there. Fania didn't understand. Neither did she know that the quarantine block was the last stop before the gas chambers and the tall chimneys of the crematoria.

Bunker 25 was dark and incredibly smelly. When her eyes had adjusted a bit, Fania could make out three-tiered bunks all along the bare walls. After a while she could see straw on those bunks and pathetic-looking women lying there, staring with lifeless eyes. Fania was horrified. The stench nearly made her faint. Someone assigned adjoining bunks to her and Clara. Panic flooded her as she lay down on the filthy straw. How long would it be before she, too, would stare with blind eyes into the darkness, waiting for death?

The door opened and a husky woman bellowed: "Madame Butterfly!" Fania's mind reeled. Was someone looking for an opera singer in this hellish place? Clara grabbed her arm and warned her that this might be a trick, but Fania had already jumped from her bunk and placed herself before the large woman. The big woman stopped shouting, looked down on Fania and motioned her to follow.

She led the way to another section of the camp, called Camp B and stopped before a hut that looked alarmingly like the one Fania had just left. But when her guide opened the door and shoved her inside, she gasped with surprise. This bunker was bright, clean, and warm and smelled of normal people. Young women in skirts and sweaters sat around a stove on real chairs, talking and laughing. Along the walls were single beds, a music stand, a piano and some other instruments. Was this a dream?

A tall, stately woman came forward and asked Fania to sing an aria from the popular opera, "Madame Butterfly." In a daze, Fania walked over to the piano and began to accompany herself to the aria "Un Bel Di." She sang with all her soul. When she came to the last note, an SS woman who had entered while Fania was singing ordered her to begin again. At last Fania stopped and the SS woman, obviously pleased, said in a loud voice that Fania was "in." Her heart leaped. Whatever "in" meant, it must be better than going back to bunker 25.

Bunker 25! Clara! She quickly told the SS woman that she would only stay if Clara could audition as well, hoping in her heart that Clara's voice would be good. To her amazement, the SS ordered Clara to be fetched from her barrack and accepted her on the strength of Fania's recommendation. Then she demanded that the two "get dressed" and marched out of the room.

The other inmates gathered around the two newcomers, asking questions and giving information all at once. Fania extracted from the chatter that she was now in the music block of Auschwitz-Birkenau and that she and Clara had just become members of the camp's women's orchestra.

The orchestra had been the idea of Auschwitz camp commandant Rudolf Hoess. He was proud of his macabre creation. The first orchestra had consisted of a few random players who played marches every morning and evening when the endless columns of unfortunate women were marched in and out of Auschwitz for forced labor. The first conductor had been a Polish prisoner by the name of Tchaikowska, a descendant of the great composer. Soon, Josef Kramer, the commandant of Birkenau Camp B, became intrigued with this unique idea and moved the orchestra to Birkenau, to the present music block. He assigned two SS women, Maria Mandel and Irma Grese to the music block, demoted Tchaikowska and made Alma Rosé conductor. She was a niece of the great composer and conductor Gustav Mahler. The group grew to 47 women, all of them taken off transports from the four corners of Europe. There were musicians from France, Greece, Holland, Belgium, Poland, Russia, and Germany. Some were Jewish, many were not. The Jewish members had their hair shaved and wore the yellow triangle, while the others were allowed to keep their hair but still had to wear identifying patches.

Fania listened carefully and was glad for the information, but now she was curious to learn how she had gotten into the group. Apparently one of the members had seen her arrive, remembered hearing her sing in Paris, and had begged Alma Rosé to send for her. Once SS officers accepted her and Clara, they were safe. And what, Fania wanted to know, was the orchestra's function now? The orchestra still played march music for the morning and evening routines. In addition, they were expected to play any time they were ordered to by the SS: for the inmates in the camp square or at any other location; for the SS at any time and place at their demand. And the SS wanted to hear real concerts, not marches, and expected concert-level performances. A poor performance, a false note, could condemn one player or the whole group to death.

And what, Fania asked, was the composition of the orchestra? A combination of 10 violins, a flute, reed pipes, 2 accordions, 3 guitars, 5 mandolins, a drum and some cymbals. How did they get musical scores for such a strange combination? That, her new comrades told her, was the big problem. Alma improvised as best she could. Fania said that she knew how to orchestrate. Everyone cheered, even the reserved Alma. Alma handed Fania paper and pencils and the score of Suppé's "Lustspiel" and begged her to adapt the score for their orchestra. Suppé was the Germans' favorite composer, she explained. A concert of his music would win the group their jailers' pleasure.

Throughout the long winter of 1944, Fania sat in the music block working at her peculiar task. Every day Alma rehearsed the group with Fania's adapted scores and day and night the women played for their gaunt, apathetic fellow prisoners. Sundays, when the SS demanded music, the orchestra played in the sauna, a huge, cold, concrete sorting center at the far end of Camp B near the open pits where the corpses were burned. In this most hellish of all places on earth, before an audience of half-dead prisoners and well-groomed SS men and women, this absurd camp orchestra played Fania's versions of Strauss and Léhar waltzes, Schubert songs, and Beethoven symphonies.

Evenings, after selection and gassing were completed for the day, the SS would come to the music block to be entertained: Schumann's "Reverie" for SS Captain Kramer, the man who was eventually known as the Beast of Bergen-Belsen; "The Charge of the Light Brigade" for Dr. Mengele, the man who decided who should live and who should die. For Frau Mandel, Fania had to sing an aria from "Madame Butterfly." Fania loathed the absurdity of this place.

From her worktable in the music block Fania could see the incoming transports. The railroad tracks had been extended into camp and the newly arriving victims no longer had to walk from the Auschwitz station. Nor were they transported any longer in those deceptive red cross trucks. As they tumbled from the cattle cars only 50 yards from Fania's window, they could hear the orchestra practicing. Fania saw them lift their heads, surprise and hope in some eyes. "Unhappy people!" thought Fania. "In another minute you will experience your first selection, you will be passing before the camp physician Dr. Mengele who, with a wave of his riding crop, will decide your fate." Fania yearned to run out to them and scream the truth of Birkenau into their faces. But she didn't dare be seen on the camp roads during *Blocksperre*!

Blocksperre—the command to stay inside the barracks —was called for two reasons. When there was an incoming transport, the roads were kept open so that victims could be moved to the gas chambers in an orderly fashion; and for camp selections. The curfew was announced with a shrill whistle which made every inmate's heart freeze. As they ran to their bunkers and stood at attention, the SS drove through the camp, bursting into the huts, selecting hundreds of victims for the ovens.

Black smoke from the crematoria hung over the camp. The stench of burning flesh permeated Fania's nostrils. It was summer in Auschwitz-Birkenau, but no budding trees announced its arrival. Only oppressive heat gave evidence of the change of season. Some time during that summer the camp roads were filled with gravel to cover the perpetual Auschwitz mud. The SS commanded Alma to prepare a special concert. A high-ranking visitor was coming to Auschwitz. The orchestra practiced intensely.

Reichsfuehrer Heinrich Himmler, second in command to Hitler himself, the man in charge of Germany's Solution to the Jewish Question, architect of this horrid camp and originator of the gas chambers, was coming to inspect his work. The orchestra was to play "The Merry Widow" for him. Fania stood no more than 20 feet from the monster himself. Once again, she became aware of the absurd, preposterous life to which she was clinging. She hoped that she would come out of this place alive so that she could tell the world of the infamy of Auschwitz.

On November 2, 1944, a cold and wet evening, Fania, Clara and most of their friends went to the sauna at the end of the camp for a shower. Fania was suddenly aware of how thin the formerly chubby Clara had become. Clara in turn remarked that Fania's hair had grown back—snow white. On the way back to their barracks, with wet towels on their heads, shivering in their rags, they were stopped by SS men snug in their warm uniforms, guns drawn. They were marched to the railroad platform near the music block and pushed into waiting boxcars. Overhead, planes crossed the dark sky. The women thought they heard bombs exploding in the distance. After traveling two days, standing crushed together in the wet train without anything to eat or drink or a chance to relieve themselves, they were ordered out into a forest. Those who could walk stumbled for two hours in the freezing rain until they came to a desolate place, their "new camp." Fania looked around. She saw nothing, no camp, no barracks, not even the SS, only some army soldiers standing around. One of them gave Fania and her group a tarpaulin tent and told the women to use it as their shelter. He said that they were now in Bergen-Belsen. Nine hours later, after setting up the tent, they crawled into it, exhausted and hungry. When they woke up in the morning, they realized that 11 members of the music group were there. Frightened, they vowed to cling together.

The soldiers gave them wooden planks and told them to build their own barracks. They labored until something with a roof was finished. After a while, SS officers from Auschwitz-Birkenau showed up: Kramer, Grese, but not Mengele. Here at Bergen-Belsen, death made its own selection. Typhus, hunger, and cold killed the inmates. Those who could still walk were marched to work, barefoot, either to dig ditches in the forest or to do heavy labor in a nearby factory. Overburdened, without food or sanitation, they slowly became animals. The winter dragged on. They celebrated New Year's 1945, with a turnip someone had stolen from a passing truck.

In April 1945, Fania, too, caught typhus. She lay semiconscious in her own excrement, her head a mass of pain. She was too weak to keep her eyes open, floating in layers of fog and pain. Was she dead already? A faraway voice was saying something, other voices persisted: "The English are here!" Is that what they were saying? Fania tried to concentrate, to listen to the unfamiliar noises and voices, but it was hard. Much better to drift off into the fog. Again someone was saying something. "Sing, Fania, sing for your English friends!" And then a red-haired, freckled soldier lifted her out of her filth and carried her outside into the spring air. Someone handed her a microphone and begged her to sing for the British Broadcasting Corporation. Strength flowed through her. She was reborn. She sang the French national anthem—the "Marseillaise." She sang "God save the King." She sang the "Internationale" and she grew stronger with every song. She knew she had survived Auschwitz, Birkenau and Bergen-Belsen.

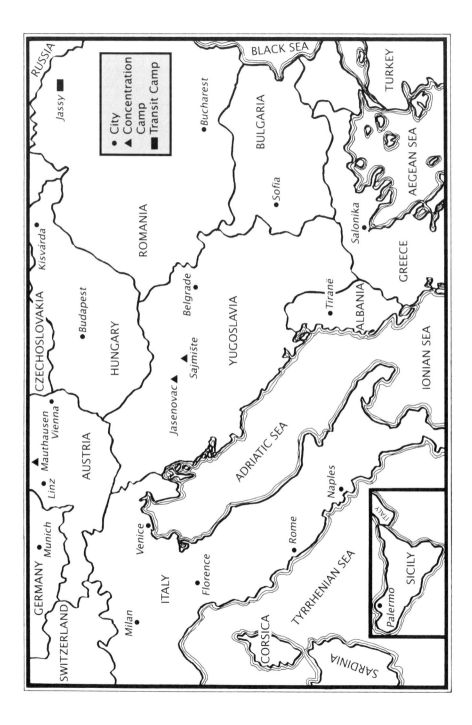

CHAPTER 7

The Balkan Countries

After France was defeated and divided, there were still two great powers in Europe that frustrated Hitler: Great Britain and the Soviet Union. He believed that he could conquer both of them and then be master of all of Europe. He expected to rule his Thousand Year Reich from the Reich's Chancellory building in Berlin and impose a "New Order" on Europe. The Germans would be the master race. Most Slavs, Serbs, all Jews and all Gypsies would be killed, either directly or by planned starvation. Only a few Slavs and Serbs would be kept alive to do slave labor.

Hitler's immediate plan was to take possession of London by August 15, 1940. At the same time, he expected to march into Moscow before winter. The English plan was coded "Operation Sea Lion." The plan to break the Soviet Union was dubbed "Barbarossa." Hitler began "Sea Lion" by trying to intimidate the British with predictions of their doom in his speeches, which he knew were heard in London. But the newly appointed prime minister, Sir Winston Churchill, declared on London radio for all the world to hear: "We have become the sole champions now in arms to defend the world cause ... We shall fight on unconquerable until the curse of Hitler is lifted from the brows of mankind."

Hitler embarked on a program of ferocious air attacks, first on the British Navy and Royal Air Force. Then, after the RAF had made a strategic air raid on Berlin in September 1940, Hitler mercilessly began bombing English cities, primarily London. But he could find no signs of submission. On the contrary, the Luftwaffe met a skilled and fearless opponent in the Royal Air Force and was up against the RAF's new invention, radar. Hitler continued the air war and added a naval blockade to starve the British and weaken their spirit. But before he could subdue the British, his attention turned to Barbarossa.

Believing that he could defeat the Soviet Union in three summer months, he planned his campaign for the spring of 1941. Hitler believed that once Soviet premier Stalin was defeated, Churchill would beg for mercy. For the time being, however, Hitler had to contend with the RAF, who were penetrating German air defenses and bombing Berlin all through the fall and winter of 1940. Hitler called these "cowardly attacks on women and children and the defenseless aged of the Reich."

Now for the first time, maneuvers other than his own dictated Hitler's next move. In October 1940, his friend and ally Mussolini sent the Italian armies east, hoping to conquer Greece as effortlessly as he had conquered Albania in the Balkans a year earlier. But the Greeks resisted and with British help, trapped Mussolini's troops in the mountains of Attica. This development turned Hitler's attention from Barbarossa to Greece: He decided to help

Mussolini and drive the British out of continental Europe at the same time. He ordered the entire German force toward the Balkans.

In preparation, Hitler arranged for a few peace treaties to smooth his way. The Balkans included five countries: Romania, Bulgaria, Yugoslavia, Albania, and Greece. Hitler invited Romania, Bulgaria, and Yugoslavia to join the Tripartite Pact of Germany, Italy and Japan. Romania and Bulgaria joined the Pact, hoping that cooperation would protect them from German aggression. Bulgaria even loaned troops to Germany to fight against Greece. Bulgaria was later rewarded for its assistance with a part of Yugoslavia.

Yugoslavia

Yugoslavia, the largest of the five Balkan countries, stretched for 100 thousand square miles from Austria to the Greek border, from the Hungarian Plains to Romania, in lovely passes of highlands and mountains. The nation was a patchwork of six historic states: Slovenia, Croatia, Bosnia and Hercegovina, Montenegro, Macedonia and Serbia. Rich in grain and tobacco, Yugoslavia had large deposits of lead and oil and was growing industrially at a fast pace. Yugoslavia's 14 million people were a mix of Serb and Macedonian Orthodox, Roman Catholics, Moslems and about 75,000 Jews. Belgrade and Zagreb had large, prosperous Jewish populations.

At first, Yugoslavia was able to stay out of the Tripartite Pact, but finally joined in March 1941. When a coup d'état resulted in a new Yugoslavian government that the Soviet Union recognized, Hitler vowed to crush Yugoslavia on his way to Greece.

In the early morning hours of April 6, 1941, the German war machine attacked Yugoslavia by ground and air. After 10 days of fierce fighting, the Yugoslav cabinet realized that their country would have to surrender. Their monarch, King Peter, and his cabinet first took refuge in Palestine, then moved to England. With Belgrade bombed to ruins, Yugoslavia capitulated on April 17. The country was carved up and divided between Germany, Italy and Bulgaria. Secret national resistance groups formed immediately under Colonels Mihailovic and Tito.

The Jews of Yugoslavia were hunted at once. More than 60,000 were caught and killed in Nazi concentration camps. Some escaped to Italy and to neighboring Bulgaria for short-lived safety.

Bulgaria

Located in the eastern part of the Balkans on the Black Sea, Bulgaria bordered Yugoslavia, Romania, Greece, and the European part of Turkey. This country was much smaller than the other Balkan nations, but it was the most industrious, and one of the richest in coal and iron deposits. Much of Bulgaria's 43,000 square miles was fertile farmland. Her 6 million people were Eastern Orthodox Catholics, Moslems, and Jews.

King Boris III of Bulgaria was married to the daughter of King Victor Emmanuel of Italy and had been a German-Italian sympathizer since the 1930s. In December 1941, Bulgaria entered the war on the side of the Germans. King Boris and his cabinet declared war on England and the United States but, paradoxically, not on Russia. Equally paradoxical were Bulgaria's actions as far as Bulgarian Jews were concerned.

Bulgaria had a long history of sheltering persecuted Jews. In the 15th century, when Jews were fleeing from the Spanish Inquisition, Bulgaria offered them asylum. There was little anti-Semitism through the centuries. When Hitler requested anti-Jewish measures to be implemented in Bulgaria and her newly acquired lands, King Boris found himself caught between his own sympathies toward the Third Reich and his country's refusal to hand over the ancient and respected Jewish community of 50,000 people for Hitler's Final Solution. The Jews did encounter social and economic deprivation, but every time a mass transport was supposed to take place, pressure was brought upon the king to call it off. Thus, the Jews of Bulgaria were not deported and extinguished. But King Boris's refusal to sacrifice the Jews did not extend beyond Bulgaria proper. The Jewish populations of Thrace and Macedonia, which were dominated by Bulgaria, were wiped out.

King Boris, who had saved the Jews of his country in spite of the fact that he was under Hitler's thumb, died suddenly in August 1943, supposedly from a heart attack. The government was reorganized and was less pro-German under the new leadership. In 1944, Bulgaria's new government announced its desire for peace with the Allies and on the 9th of September, 1944, Soviet troops entered Sofia. German dominance over Bulgaria ended.

Romania

Romania, the easternmost country of the Balkans and also the second largest, bordered on the Soviet Union, Hungary, Bulgaria, and Yugoslavia, and had access to the Black Sea. This country contained the Carpathian Mountains and Danube valleys. Romania, too, was productive in agriculture and rich in gas, oil, and coal deposits. The Romanian population of 16 million people was a mix of Germans, Hungarians, Serbs, Croats, Jews, and Gypsies.

Like its neighbors, Romania was afraid of losing its independence. In June 1940, the Soviet Union claimed the Romanian regions of Bessarabia and Bukovina. Later that year, Germany took over Transylvania and gave it to Hungary. To avoid further losses, Romania's King Carol appointed a pro-German cabinet and abdicated. His son, King Michael, formed a new government under General Ion Antonescu. In November 1940, he joined Romania to the Tripartite Pact. German troops immediately occupied Romania.

General Antonescu brought Romania into the war on the side of Germany. His army fought side by side with the Germans at Stalingrad, even when German fortune turned sour in February 1943, and the Red Army (Soviets) pushed the enemy back to the gates of Bucharest. The Romanians switched sides and overthrew Antonescu, just as the Soviet forces started to liberate Romania from German protection in August 1944.

Liberation came too late for 270,000 Jews whom the Germans—with help from the Romanians—hanged, burned, and shot. The whole Jewish community was devastated. In one three-day killing spree that began on October 23, 1941, 27,000 Jews died—men, women, and children machine-gunned in the Balkan forests and thrown into pits. And nobody objected.

Albania

Nestled between Yugoslavia, Greece, and the Adriatic Sea, Albania had been invaded by Mussolini in 1939. A year later, the Italians used the tiny state as a base for their invasion of Greece. Hitler, too, used Albania, taking wealth from the country and harassing the Albanian Moslem peasant population. From there, he joined Mussolini in Greece.

Greece

Greece, the Mediterranean member of the five Balkan states, had fought off the Italian invasion with British help. Greece and Great Britain were the only countries in Europe in 1941 that dared oppose the powerful German-Italian Axis. Together, they had been able to cope with one of the powers, but they could not hold off both.

The Germans, arrogant with victories in Yugoslavia and Albania, charged Greece on April 10, 1941—very early in the morning, as was their method. The Greek's Macedonian front collapsed within days and the Greek Second Army surrendered. Under the onslaught of German panzers and Stukas, the British withdrew their troops from mainland Greece by April 17, and from the Greek islands by April 30. The Germans, meanwhile, had penetrated to the Isthmus of Corinth by means of parachute troops. In the east, they had captured Salonika on the Aegean Sea and had begun to occupy the islands off the coast of Turkey. Hitler wanted Turkey to join the Axis and intended to offer the islands to Turkey as security against Italy, but the Turks stayed out of the war.

On April 27, the Germans drove triumphantly through the deserted streets of Athens and haughtily hoisted their swastika over the Acropolis. Greece was forced to surrender and a German tyranny set in that lasted for three harsh years. Under German oppression, Greek misfortune reached a state of national disaster. Three occupying armies—German, Italian, and Bulgarian—all demanded housing and food at Greece's expense. Before long, the Greeks starved. In Athens, people fainted in the streets from lack of food and died leaning against the corners of buildings, too weak to go on. There was no fuel, no warm clothing, and no leather for shoes. Children cried in schoolrooms from the bitter cold. People used paper wrappings to protect their hands and feet. The young and healthy were sent to Germany as workers. Jews were deported and gassed. And the conquerors lived in comfort.

King George of Greece and his government left Athens and set up an exile government in London, supporting and financing Greek resistance organizations. But as determined as these patriots were, they could not stem the destruction. In the cities, an estimated 500 thousand Greeks died from cold, hunger, and bombing. More than 1,000 Greek villages were leveled, their inhabitants killed or displaced. Entire Jewish communities were shipped to Auschwitz, still wearing their colorful native costumes. They walked into the gas chambers never comprehending the commands the Germans barked at them.

On May 20, 1941, German troops parachuted onto the island of Crete. For the first time in history, a full fighting force was air-dropped onto the scene of action, men and machinery, ready to do battle. The British inflicted over 6,000 casualties and fled. The Cretans were shocked into confusion. Ten days after the troops had landed, Crete surrendered to Hitler's force.

World Highlights, 1941-1945

Roosevelt is reelected for a third term. Trotsky assassinated in Mexico on Stalin's order. Ernest Hemingway writes For Whom the Bell Tolls. *Penicillin is mass-produced in the West and streptomycin is discovered. Japanese air force attacks Pearl Harbor, drawing the United States into World War II. Roosevelt is elected to a fourth term. Roosevelt dies; Harry Truman becomes president. Hitler commits suicide. Enrico Fermi splits the atom. Joe Louis retains world heavyweight boxing crown. Aaron Copland composes "Appalachian Spring" and Irving Berlin writes "White Christmas."* Casablanca, *starring Humphrey Bogart and Ingrid Bergman, becomes a popular film, and* Oklahoma, *a popular musical. A polio epidemic kills 1,200 in the United States and cripples thousands more. First atomic bomb is detonated near Alamogordo, New Mexico. Japan surrenders.*

NORWAY

FINLAND

SWEDEN

• Leningrad

ESTONIA

BALTIC SEA

LATVIA

Riga ★

• Moscow

LITHUANIA

RUSSIA

★ Kovino

Stutthof ▲ Danzig

• Treblinka

▲ Ravensbrück ☆

Vilna • • Minsk

▲ Sachsenhausen POLAND

WHITE

Berlin • Chelmno ☆ Warsaw

RUSSIA

GERMANY ★ Lódz'

☆ Sobibor

★ Bialystok

Gross-Rosen ★ Maidanek ☆

★ Theresienstadt Auschwitz ★ Lublin

Kiev • • Babi Yar

Prague • CZECHO ☆ ☆ Belzec

★ Kraków

UKRAINE

▲ SLOVAKIA Lvov

Mauthausen • Vienna

Kisvárda

Jassy ■■

• Odessa

AUSTRIA

• Budapest

ROMANIA

HUNGARY

Jasenovac

★ Bucharest

▲ ▲

Sajmište

BLACK SEA

Belgrade

YUGOSLAVIA Sofia

ALBANIA BULGARIA

• Tiranë Istanbul

ADRIATIC SEA

Salonika

ITALY

GREECE

TURKEY

SICILY AEGEAN SEA

Athens •

CYPRUS

IONIAN SEA

•	City
▲	Concentration Camp
■■	Transit Camp
☆	Death Camp
★	Ghetto

CHAPTER 8

War with the Soviet Union

In the eighth year of his rule and the third year of the war, at the zenith of his power and right after his successes in the Balkans, Hitler gave orders to attack the Soviet Union. On June 22, 1941, the German Army attacked that massive land.

The huge Soviet empire encompassed nearly 9 million square miles of territory and covered 11 time zones, from frozen tundra in the north to citrus-growing valleys in the south. It stretched from the Baltic Sea to the Bering Straits and from the Arctic Ocean to the Pamir Mountains in Afghanistan. The population of 170 million united in 1917 into the Union of Soviet Socialist Republics, and adopted Communism as their form of government. By 1927 Joseph Stalin, their totalitarian dictator, had made a huge concentration camp out of the country, ordering forced labor for its growing industrialization and collectivized farming for agriculture. Atheism became the official policy of the state, but many Communists remained members of the Russian Orthodox Church. There were also many Jews, Moslems, and Buddhists in the vast country.

Hitler did not want the Soviet cities nor did he like the Russian people. He planned to level the former and starve the latter. He coveted the land as Lebensraum (living room) for his future German state. But for now, he wanted and needed Russia's iron, coal, furs, and timber, and he was ready to fight for them.

His war plan called for intense action by three army groups at once. Early successes were followed by severe defeats as the winter set in. From headquarters in Berlin, Hitler demanded that Germany's positions in the Soviet Union be held at all cost. His generals chafed under the unreasonable battle orders and were blamed for the reverses. Instead of changing the orders, Hitler replaced the generals, one by one, with new military leaders who carried out his eccentric tactics.

Hitler had thought it possible to conquer the Soviet Union in three summer months. But that war in the east lasted for three years. Two Romanian armies and a division of Ukrainian soldiers fought alongside the Germans. The Germans were hindered by relentless partisan action in the Ukraine and in Belorussia; the Soviets were helped by the harsh winters in the Steppe. What gains the Germans made in their spring and summer offensives were lost in winter battles; what lands they occupied were taken back. By late 1944, the war in the east turned. At last the Soviets were driving the Germans back over their own borders and pursuing them to Berlin.

A Child's Vision of Hell: Alys's Story

Wedged between the Soviet Union and Poland is the small state of Lithuania, given to the Soviet Union in the 1939 German-Soviet Pact. In this Pact, Hitler promised

Stalin parts of Poland if Stalin would not interfere in Germany's assault on Poland. The Red Army occupied this country in 1940. But in 1941, on his way toward the Soviet Union, Hitler invaded the tiny country because it lay in his path to Moscow and Leningrad. German troops swept the Red Army out and settled into Lithuania for five years of occupation. Ruthless damage was done to cities and countryside; Lithuanians were terribly abused, whether or not they were Jewish. Countless men, some with their families, were dragged to German labor camps.

The Stanké family of Kaunas owned and operated the city's official radio station. They lived on a large estate in one of the suburbs. The family consisted of the father, a mother of White Russian ancestry, Aunt Lyudunia, and two boys, Lus, age 10 and Alys, 6. The Stankés were pious Catholics.

In June 1940, the Soviets occupied Lithuania, holding the country in a grip of terror. No one was safe. People stayed in their houses, fear and resentment in their hearts. Mothers warned children sternly not to go into town.

In the summer, Alys and a friend played around the estate. But one day they ran to Bytauto Park, in town. As they neared the park they heard horses approaching from the far side of the street and could hear the wild shouts of the riders. They hurried toward the park entrance and reached it at the same time as the pack of wild riders. They hid behind a tree.

The horde stampeded past them, filling the wide street, trampling to death men and women in their path. Wild-eyed, foaming horses stomped so closely by the tree that Alys could see the short, dark-skinned men who rode them, could see their eyes, hear their sabres clanging and smell the sharp odor of their horses. "Mongols!" whispered a man near them. Terrified, the boys clung to each other and ran home as soon as they could.

As the warm weather changed to cool days and cold nights, the Soviets made plans to move into Alys's house. They gave his father six hours' notice to get out. Six hours to find another place, pack, and move. Depressed, angry, and powerless against the tyrants, Alys's mother and his Aunt Lyudunia filled boxes and bags with their necessities while Father went into town to look for rooms. All their handsome furniture, rugs, silver, valuable paintings, and all of Alys's toys and books had to be left behind.

The war dragged on. The Stanké family changed. Alys's father and mother became thinner and grayer, Lus, quieter. But Alys worried the family most of all. He grew pale and thin, refusing to eat. Finally, his mother decided to send him to her sister in the country.

For a short while he led the carefree life of a seven-year-old, picking berries, taking walks and listening to Mr. Petras, the caretaker, tell stories and sing Lithuanian folksongs. One day they were walking in the cemetery when they saw a big Russian truck approach. Mr. Petras quickly lifted Alys up into the branches of a large tree and climbed up after him. Below them, three soldiers with red armbands got out of the truck and dragged four unshaven men in shirtsleeves out onto the gravel, their hands tied behind their backs. Mr. Petras recognized the men as Lithuanian freedom fighters. The soldiers beat the men viciously, first with their hands, then with rifle butts. In the end they shot them. As Alys and Mr. Petras watched in numb horror, the soldiers buried their victims and drove away in a burst of fumes and gravel. The nightmarish scene tormented Alys day and night. He was happy when his aunt sent him back to Kaunas.

All through the winter of 1940 and the following spring, fear of deportation haunted the family. Men were rounded up on the streets, routed out of their homes, tortured, and sent to forced labor in Siberia. Often, whole families went. Alys stayed awake at night, listening for the collection trucks.

Incredibly, in the summer of 1941, the Soviets left. Was the war over? Was Lithuania free? A new army arrived: handsome, clean young men in shiny boots and snug uniforms. The people of Kaunas lined the streets, threw flowers at the newcomers and shouted "Victory!" Euphoria lasted for three whole days. On the fourth day, the SS arrived and settled into the country as the new usurpers, making their presence felt everywhere. At school, Stalin's picture came down and Hitler's went up. The raised-fist salute was replaced with the outstretched arm. And there were changes in town, too. It was now forbidden to leave town without permission, or even to leave one's house overnight without a pass. Why were people arrested for wearing sunglasses or having a beard? Why were boys forbidden to run? That was the decree Alys minded the most.

Air raids interrupted his sleep. Almost every night, the Soviets dropped bombs and parachutists. All too often, they were caught and the Germans hung them in public at Azuolyno Park. The citizens of Kaunas were forced to watch the hangings. Children, too, had to attend.

Alys knew nothing but war and killing. One afternoon, while waiting for his aunt, he noticed a group of men digging a ditch. He saw them put away their shovels and line up in a row, facing the ditch. As Alys watched and listened in growing terror, he heard a command, then rifle shots, and saw the men drop into the pit. A new group stepped forward. Alys was terrified. An SS man strolled by and motioned him away, saying lightly: "Only Jews!" Despite the ban on running, Alys dashed away, searching in fear for his aunt.

Years passed. Hunger and cold were Alys's only companions. At age 10, Alys was no longer a child. All around him, men were being rounded up and sent to forced labor in Germany. Whole families disappeared in street raids. In the summer of 1944, in a house-to-house roundup, the Germans took the Stanké family prisoners.

They found themselves in a labor camp near Berlin called Bugk. Alys, too young to work, was sent to a German school. His troubles started right away, when he refused to raise his arm in the "Heil Hitler" morning salute. Soon, he was asked to become a member of the Hitler Youth. He refused, despite beatings. Finally, he was thrown out of the German school.

Early in 1945, Alys heard the grown-ups say that the front was moving closer. Suddenly one cold day in January, the prisoners of war were moved again. They traveled for days, stacked up against each other in an overcrowded train. When the train stopped for air raids, many prisoners escaped into the night. Alys's father, too, considered escaping with his family. But where would they go? How far would they get, weak and tattered as they all were?

They finally arrived at what seemed to be their destination, a camp near Bitterfeld where, it seemed, half of Europe was represented. They heard rumors that this was the place from where the Germans selected prisoners for medical experiments. When they were informed that they would be moved again, Alys's father turned pale with fear.

The next stop was Würzburg in southern Germany. This time they had to build their own barracks. Alys's father worked as hard as he could, grateful that the rumors he had heard had not been true.

On March 16, 1945, leaflets were dropped from airplanes onto the city. Alys read them to his parents in flawless German: The city was going to be bombed by the Allies! The SS laughed and declared the announcement enemy propaganda. Yet they were the first to head for the bomb shelters when low-flying, silvery formations appeared on the horizon.

After a long time, the drone of the planes began to fade and the all-clear siren wailed. Alys and Lus crawled out of the shelter into a smoke-filled dawn. Below them, Würzburg burned, the centuries-old castle crumbling as they stared. The boys took advantage of the chaos and ran into the devastated town. Someone was distributing food and the two hungry boys eagerly got in line. With sandwiches in their pockets, they ran back to the barracks and shared the food with their parents. Even before they could get back, the sirens sounded again.

Alys dove into a crater hole just as the bombs started to hit the trembling ground again. The pressure flattened him against the base of the crater. His eardrums nearly burst and his mouth filled with dirt. When it was all over, he was surprised to still be alive.

The bombing of Würzburg continued for two weeks. Alys, recovered from his fear of dying as soon as the shelling stopped, continued to run into town for food. He was glad that he had learned to speak German. He could simply pose as a displaced German boy begging for food for his bombed-out family.

In the early morning hours of April 3, 1945, Alys saw American tanks driving through Würzburg and up the hill to his barracks. They planted an American flag in the yard! Alys stood hypnotized by that waving flag. So this is what freedom looks like, he thought. A few weeks later, the Stanké family was repatriated to France. From there, young Alys eventually made his way to Canada.

Biography of a Partisan: Bryna's Ordeal

Ukraine, the large territory between Poland, Romania and Russia, open to the Black Sea on its southern border, became a thoroughfare for German troops on their way to Moscow. In the five years that the theater of war played itself out there, the country was ravaged. But because of thick forests and closeness to Russia, Ukraine became a stronghold for anti-German partisans who took their orders from the Red Army. They hindered the Germans and plagued them whenever and wherever they could. In return, German wrath was fierce and few partisans lived to tell the harrowing tales of their ordeal.

Among the partisans were many Jews who had fled to the woods to hide from the Nazis. They, too, joined the freedom fighters. Jews were in particular danger, and not only from the Nazis: They were also persecuted by the Ukrainians and by the Russians. Among those who survived to tell her story was Bryna.

Bryna was born in 1925 in Baranowicze, close to the Russo-Polish border. Before she was five years old, her parents moved to the *shtetl* of Byten where they brought up their four daughters: Yentl, Henia, Dalya, and Bryna.

An older son, Nathan, had already left for America. A younger son, Chaim, was born in the shtetl.

The shtetl—a village predominantly inhabited by Jews —offered security and identity and the chance to observe Jewish laws and customs. During the week, the Jews worked hard, but also enjoyed Klezmer music, dancing, and Yiddish plays. Every Friday afternoon, shops, work-rooms, and music halls closed. The smell of that holiday delicacy, *cholent*, was everywhere and Jews went home to enjoy the Sabbath. Around the festive table, strangers shared the *gefilte fish* (chopped patties) and *kugel* (noodle pudding) while Sabbath prayers and singing resounded from the synagogue and from every house along the narrow streets. The only Gentiles in the shtetl were the mayor, the postmaster, the police, and a few teachers. The only outside contact for the Jews was with farmers who brought their harvest into the shtetl on market days. After the produce was sold and before going back to their farms, the peasants would get drunk and insult and torment the Jews. Thus, even in their isolation, the Jews of Byten were well aware of Polish and Russian anti-Semitism.

In September 1939, after Hitler had taken Poland, hundreds of fleeing Jews arrived in Byten with reports of German cruelty and brutality. Byten heard, but did not believe; the Jews listened, but did not comprehend. Before the Germans reached the shtetl, the Russians arrived with tanks and trucks, a new local government and a se-cret police. Outside the village, cattle cars stood ready to take anti-Russians to Siberia. In the shtetl, Jewish organizations dissolved, social and cultural life stopped. The Jews, at first glad to see the Russians instead of the Germans, soon learned to fear them. Russian occupation lasted for two frightful years, but when the Russians left Byten on June 22, 1941, and German soldiers and SS troops arrived in their place, chaos broke out. Germany was at war with Russia. What would become of the Jews of Byten?

At first they were ordered to do hard labor, even little Chaim. Then came the order to form a Jewish council, a Judenrat, whose first task was to herd all Jews into a small area of 48 houses enclosed by barbed wire. They were to form a ghetto with 20 people to a single room. Food rations were cut in half, the smell of cholent was only a memory. On July 25, 1942, the ghetto of Byten was liquidated. Almost all of the 1,200 Jews were massacred. After the killers left, the looters came.

When the ghetto was finally still, a few survivors crawled from hiding places, among them Bryna, her sisters Dalya and Yentl, and Yentl's two children. Bryna resolved that she would flee the devastated place and hide in the forest. She had heard of a group of partisans who were hiding out there. She decided to try to join them and at least die fighting. She persuaded her sisters to join her.

Eventually the five of them arrived in a Communist stronghold called Wolcze Nory—the wolves' nest—a den of resistance in the dense forest in the midst of the German occupation. They were assigned to a camp unit directly under the leadership of the Red Army. Bryna understood quickly that the Wolcze Nory stronghold was part of a larger Communist underground operation in the forests of the Polish and Russian Ukraine, in the dense woods that covered much of the territory of White Russia. Beyond the woods to the north lay Moscow, from where the orders came to the partisans. Among themselves, the partisans exchanged messages and information between forest camps by messengers crossing the thick forest on footpaths and hidden dirt roads known to them alone. She saw that the freedom fighters at Wolcze Nory were well equipped with guns and rifles. Some carried cartridge belts hung loosely over their shoulders. Their leader instructed them in resistance warfare and assigned them to a place three miles from the main camp where they had to build their own hut from twigs and bark. They were told to get a cow—any way they could—and were charged with cooking and caring for the whole Wolcze Nory compound. Because there were children among the hundred or so partisans in Bryna's group, their camp was soon known as the family camp. They seemed safe for the moment.

In the fall of 1942, the Germans, desperate from their defeat in Moscow, mounted an offensive against the partisans in the forests around Moscow. On September 18, they ambushed the woods in great numbers, harassing the freedom fighters with low-flying planes and penetrating the partisans' defenses with tanks. Orders from Moscow were that partisans intensify sabotage operations, prepare for a major attack, and be ready to flee at a moment's notice.

At Bryna's camp, they all knew their assignments, but when the first onslaught of German troops and armored vehicles came crashing through the trees, organization broke down. The central executive staff and the commander in chief left to set up defenses deeper in the woods and Bryna and the people from the family camp fled deep into the forest. Bryna felt desperate. How would they manage with crying children? How would they feed them and keep them warm at night? More urgently, how would they run with small children through this inhospitable terrain?

The morning dawned hot and humid. As they fled ever deeper into the woods, they passed the mutilated bodies of their comrades, under trees, in groves, everywhere. As Bryna hurried past them she saw their tortured features, their twisted or missing limbs. She sent a fervent prayer to Heaven: God, let me and my sisters be shot! Let Yentl and the babies die before we can be captured and tortured like this!

Yentl and the children fell behind. The leader stopped the fleeing group and asked the mothers to camp in a nearby hollow with their children. Someone would fetch them the next day.

The next morning, as Bryna rushed to the hollow, five mothers came toward her, five dead babies in their arms. Bryna, weak-kneed, searched for Yentl: What in God's name had happened? Ashen, Yentl told a story of madness. One of the mothers, in a fit of despair, had taken her shawl and slowly suffocated the infant at her breast and, as if infected by an inexplicable hysteria, one mother after another slowly smothered the baby in her arms. Yentl had implored them to stop, to come to their senses, but they did not hear her.

Shouts of "Halt! Halt!" echoed around them; they had to move on. Bryna took the baby boy from her sister Yentl's arms, pressed him to her own bosom and firmly grasped the hand of his sister, Rochelle. She urged the uncomprehending child along with little songs and rhymes while holding the baby ever tighter. Behind them, gunfire reverberated through the woods. By sunset they had run 15 miles. Exhausted and terribly hungry,

Bryna fell in a heap into some dry leaves, the baby still in her arms.

The baby looked so small and white. Bryna looked closer in the waning light and felt the blood turn cold in her veins. The little boy was dead. In her flight from the demons behind her, she had suffocated her sister's child. She was inconsolable.

They tried to get back to their camp at Wolcze Nory, but ran straight into a gunfire attack. Smoke and erupting earth was so thick around them that they soon lost each other. After the attack quieted down, Bryna found her group, but Yentl and her little girl were missing. Bryna prayed that they were only lost and had joined up with another group. But six months later, a fellow partisan told her that he had come upon corpses of women and children along the road to Kochanowo. Bryna asked him to take her there. She recognized Yentl and Rochelle among the dead and asked her friend to help her bury them. They concealed all the cadavers and stood to say the *El Molei Rachamin* (Merciful God), the traditional Jewish prayer for the dead. Bryna lifted her eyes from the blood-soaked earth to the trees above her. Where was this merciful God?

The weather was turning cold. Soon, it would be 1943, and they were still running. Bryna's group made their way back to Byten hoping to find shelter and food for the winter. They dug a cave with their bare hands and camouflaged it with green moss. They needed water and hurried to dig a well before the ground froze. Then they foraged for food and found a potato field nearby. At night, Bryna and a few other members would steal potatoes and cook them in the cave, hoping that the smell would not betray them. Once the snow began to fall, they had to take care not to leave footprints lest the Germans would find them. Thus they struggled into spring, hoping and praying that the war would end. In the spring they returned once more to the forest, not dreaming that they would have to remain there for another long year before liberation finally came to Ukraine. All during that summer they worked with non-Jewish partisans to do violence to the common enemy: derailing trains, destroying tracks, disrupting telephone lines. By March 1944, an enemy of quite a different kind attacked Bryna: She contracted typhus. Burning with high fever and at the same time shivering with chills, she faced death for 14 days. When she at last recovered, she was skin and bones, completely bald, and had to learn to walk again.

In July the woods were again full of Germans but now the Germans themselves were hiding from the pursuing Red Army. Russian tanks were driving the once mighty Germans back toward Germany. The long and savage occupation in Ukraine was over.

CHAPTER 9

Italy and Hungary

Italy

Italy was one of the last countries in Europe to experience Nazi abuse. Italy had been dominated since 1922 by a fascist leader, the Duce Benito Mussolini. Mussolini had allowed King Victor Emmanuel to remain a figurehead ruler with little power while Mussolini actually ruled the country autocratically. But in July 1943, the Italian Grand Council deposed the fascist dictator and King Victor Emmanuel was once again Italy's sole ruler. The hated Mussolini was taken to a mountaintop hotel as prisoner of the Italians. Because Mussolini was Hitler's friend and ally, Hitler met at once with his staff to plan a rescue.

On September 13, 1943, German gliders landed on the mountain, took the guards prisoner, stuffed the overweight Duce into one of the gliders and delivered him to Hitler's Berlin headquarters. The German plan had also called for the arrest of King Victor Emmanuel and the Grand Council, but king and council had fled from Rome to the safety of southern Italy and the Allies. Hitler's personal bodyguard took the Duce back to Italy, installed him in a northern Italian village from where he again ruled the land, guarded by the bodyguards and beholden to Hitler.

Meanwhile, German troops successfully fought against the Allies in the south of Italy, holding them as far as possible from the Reich and placing the whole of northern Italy under German occupation. SS Sturmführer Karl Wolff became Hitler's representative in Rome and the Jews came under the power of Sturmführer Theodor Dannecker, a deputy of Adolf Eichmann.

Jews had flourished in Italy since the destruction of the Jerusalem Temple in AD 70, the time of the Roman Empire. During the Middle Ages, Italian cities contained some of the richest and most ornate synagogues in all the world. In modern Italy, Jews were integrated citizens and did not experience anti-Semitism. Even Mussolini had not persecuted the Jews, never yielding to Hitler's pressure for active anti-Semitic measures. In the fall of 1943, Hitler marched in and the Jews were told what to expect. They did not believe the reports of German inhumanities and very few of them fled their ancestral homes. In the two years of German occupation, Jews were uprooted, their homes taken over by the Nazis. Their magnificent synagogues were smashed to ruins, holy treasures taken away. In Pisa, Nazis murdered a *minyan* (a group of 10 Jews gathered for prayer) in a private home. In Rome, right under the windows of the pope, the roundups were conducted with such cruelty that Christian spectators fled in horror. The terror stopped only when Allied troops entered Rome and took control of Italy on April 29, 1945. By then, 17,000 of Italy's 50,000 Jews were dead.

Hungary

Hitler's fortunes had been declining ever since the siege of Stalingrad in 1943. Meanwhile, the Allied forces had grown in strength. In June 1944, American armies came to Europe's rescue, but before they could smash the German war machine, one last country in Europe fell victim to the full force of Hitler's fury.

Hungary had been ruled by Attila the Hun 1,500 years earlier. Magyar tribes settled there after Attila left, leaving no other trace but his name. The Magyars built Hungary into one of Europe's most productive sources of grains and grapes, established some of Europe's most sophisticated cities, nurtured some of the world's greatest artists like the playwright, Ferenc Molnar and the musician, Franz Liszt. Magyars also ruthlessly suppressed the Slavs and vetoed reforms in the Austro-Hungarian Empire at the beginning of the 20th century. In the 1930s, Hungary developed a fascist movement which followed the Nazi pattern of racism. Hitler brought the 9.5 million inhabitants of Hungary under Nazi rule in his last year of power.

In 1940 the Hungarian regent Miklos Horthy had already committed his country to Germany when he joined the Berlin-Rome-Tokyo Tripartite Pact. A year later, Hungary allowed German troops to move through her territory on their way to attack Yugoslavia. In June 1941, Hungarian troops joined Germany in the invasion of the Soviet Union. Hungary was rewarded by the Reich with part of Czechoslovakia and territories in Transylvania. But Horthy became disillusioned with Hitler and began to sympathize with Stalin instead. Hitler summoned the Hungarian ruler to Berlin and informed him that he would have to accept the Hungarian Nazi Dome Sztojay as premier of Hungary and that, henceforth, German troops would be stationed in Budapest. Furthermore, Horthy would have to hand over the Jews of Hungary for extinction. Horthy agreed to all propositions. Once back in Budapest, however, he broke off the alliance with Germany. The Germans forced him to step down and on October 16, 1944, he was deported to Austria. He lived there quietly until the Americans liberated him in 1945. Meanwhile, Premier Sztojay carried out Hitler's orders in regard to the Jews.

Wearing the yellow star came first. Then, in April 1944, Jews in the provinces were forced from their homes and crammed into ghettos. From there they were shipped to Auschwitz and were quickly killed. After the rural areas were free of Jews, Sztojay tackled the large and prosperous Jewish community of Budapest. The roundups began. Cattle cars packed with Jews traveled to Auschwitz. The Jews were gassed on arrival, their bodies burned in haste by the tens of thousands. Finally, the Hungarian government balked and supported one of its Jewish citizens, the influential lawyer Resco Kastner, in his efforts to save the remaining Jews of Hungary. Kastner approached Heinrich Himmler through Himmler's deputy Kurt Becher and, backed by his government and the Swiss Joint Distribution Committee, negotiated the release of the Jews.

Kastner had a measure of success. Himmler granted the release of 9,000 Jews from Hungary to Vienna so they could be shown to the representatives of the Joint Distribution Committee as an example of German humanity. In August 1944, an additional 3,000 Joint Jews were released from Bergen-Belsen concentration camp and sent to Switzerland. But 200,000 others—half the Jewish community of Hungary—died in Auschwitz. The gas chambers and the ovens were so busy that not all could be killed. As the Russians approached Auschwitz in January of 1945, those still alive were sent on death marches, driven on foot, ahead of the Allies, from place to place in the cold winter. Not many survived that barbarous trek.

Isabella's Memory of the Death March

Isabella Katz's childhood and youth were spent happily in a small Hungarian town called Kisvárda. She had five sisters and a brother. She became familiar with anti-Jewish attitudes when people began to call her and her siblings "dirty Jews" and her friends excluded her from their plays and parties. But nothing had prepared Isabella for life in the ghetto and she wished with all her heart that she could leave it behind.

On a Monday in May of 1944, she did. Cattle cars stood ready at the railroad station in Kisvárda, ready to take the Jews out of the ghetto. Isabella was glad. Nothing, she thought, could be as bad as this depressing, smelly ghetto. But after she had been in the crowded cattle car for three horrid days without food or water, without a toilet, yearning for a breath of fresh air, after she had seen people get sick next to her and watched an old man die in the car, she thought again, "After this suffocating ride is over, nothing, nothing can be worse than this."

The train finally stopped. The sign at the station proclaimed *Oswiecim:* Auschwitz. Ahead of her, selection was already taking place. Someone whispered the name Mengele. Isabella was shoved and pushed ever closer to that man. When they all stood in front of him, he ordered

Mama to one side, her brother to the men's prison and, incredibly, Potya, her little sister, to be thrown into an open pit together with other children from the transport. Mama no longer saw this tragedy—she was already moving toward her own death by gassing and burning—but Isabella was dazed. Was this reality? Isabella was still looking into the fiery pit without comprehension when she and her three other sisters were pushed onward, away from the spectacle, to the far end of camp and into showers. Hardly aware of what was going on, they were lined up, robbed of their possessions, shaved even to the pubic hair, tattooed with a number and rushed to Block 10.

They managed to stay together through the summer of 1944 and into the winter. They endured heat and cold, hunger and hard labor, but they stayed together. They were unaware that the war was going badly for the Germans. When the Russians got closer, the inmates were penned into cattle cars on an icy night in December and taken to a labor camp in eastern Germany. And as the Russians kept coming, they were uprooted again.

On January 22, 1945, Isabella and her sisters became part of a Death March. About a thousand inmates who were still alive were rounded up. Now there was not even the luxury of a cattle car. Five abreast, they stumbled, weak and broken, through the snow toward Bergen-Belsen, just ahead of the Red Army.

Isabella had grown so weak that it took extra-human effort to keep walking. It was tempting to step out of line and just lie at the side of the road for a few minutes—but those who did were shot and left to die. Isabella, hungry and cold to a point where she could feel nothing, stumbled on for the sake of her sisters. Only when the column halted at night did the four sisters dare to fall exhausted into a haystack in someone's barn.

They pushed on, the next day and the day following. How many days, how many hours, could they endure this inhuman march? On January 23, a blizzard raged. A few prisoners managed to escape, but many were lying dead by the road, shot through the head. Again, they were whipped into rows of five. SS men walked briskly in their shining boots and ready rifles. Ahead and in back of each column, the SS men patrolled as the pitiful prisoners trudged through the snow, through German towns and villages where no one ever remembered seeing them. One of the sisters saw what looked like a deserted house —no smoke rose from the chimney, no dog in the doghouse, no sign of life near the barn. In a moment of insight she rushed out of the line toward that doghouse. Isabella and one other sister followed her. The three crouched first inside the dog's hut, then in back of it in the deep snow, hiding from the passing column. Would the SS notice their escape? Would they be shot? What would the bullet feel like? Would they die immediately? But the SS walked past them. The sisters fell into each other's arms.

The three crawled into the farmhouse. Miraculously, it was indeed empty. But the refrigerator was full! Isabella ate and ate until she was sick. She slept and slept in a soft bed upstairs. She woke up and ate again. On January 25, tanks rumbled under the farmhouse windows. Soldiers waved red flags. Red flags! At last, the sisters were liberated by the Russian Army!

Later they learned that their fourth sister was dragged to Bergen-Belsen, was liberated by the British but died soon after liberation. Their brother survived many concentration camps, and was finally liberated by the Americans, but also died in their care.

World Highlights 1946-1950

George Orwell writes Animal Farm; *Sartre writes* Les Chemins de la Liberté. *Benjamin Spock's* Baby and Child Care *becomes best seller. South Pole expedition of R.E. Byrd takes place. Popular songs are: "Come Rain or Come Shine," "Buttons and Bows," "Riders in the Sky," and "Rudolph the Red-Nosed Reindeer." Gandhi is assassinated. Harry S. Truman is president of the United States. Cole Porter writes "Kiss Me, Kate" and Arthur Miller writes "Death of a Salesman." Long-playing record albums are invented. Babe Ruth dies. Joe Louis retires. Orwell's latest book is* 1984. *Plutonium is separated from pitchblende concentrates. Einstein publishes the "General Field Theory." Miltown comes into use as tranquilizer. Antihistamines become popular remedy for colds and allergies. India becomes a sovereign state. Cortisone is discovered. The Jewish State of Israel comes into existence. North Korea invades South Korea.*

Sentencing

With Germany's unconditional surrender to the victorious Allies on May 8, 1945, 12 years of Nazi rule ended. An inquisition into public guilt began. An International Military Tribunal was created and held court at Nüremberg from September 1945 to October 1946. A British court sprang up at Lüneburg and dealt with Nazis caught by English liberators. Formerly occupied nations set for themselves the task of judging those who were responsible for war crimes and for crimes against humanity. German courts, under orders from the victorious Allies, embarked on denazification programs. A *Volksgericht*—a people's court—formed in Vienna. Countries all over Europe, freed at last from the German presence, judged their oppressors. But many a corrupt German slipped through the net of justice, either to safety in South America or under false pretenses to a new life in North America. Many Nazi officials slipped quietly back into the mainstream of life in Germany, returning to wives and children, desks and shops, never to talk or perhaps even think, of the past. Like sheep, these Germans had obeyed any order, had done any contemptible deed upon the slightest command, and they considered themselves guiltless; perhaps thinking, let those who gave the orders be judged, not them.

Top Nazis had avoided the judges by killing themselves: Hitler was dead, so was Himmler and many other high ranking killers whose names do not appear in the pages of this book. Here, I report only on the fates of those whose names are mentioned in these pages.

Ion Antonescu, the pro-German Marshal of Romania, was tried and sentenced, and executed in his own country in 1946.

Werner Best, SS Commissioner for occupied Denmark, was tried before a Danish tribunal, sentenced to death in 1948; sentence changed to imprisonment; he was released in 1951.

Fedor von Bock, Commander of Army Group Center, was killed in an air raid in 1945 before he could be brought to trial.

Theodor Dannecker, SS Sturmfuehrer in charge of Jewish deportation in France, later in Bulgaria and Italy, was reported missing as late as 1967.

Adolf Eichmann of the Office For The Final Solution Of The Jewish Question, fled to South America, was recognized and kidnapped by Israeli agents, tried and executed in Jerusalem in 1960.

Alexander von Falkenhausen, Military Commander for occupied Belgium, was sentenced by a Belgian court to 12 years in prison, but was released in 1951.

Hans Frank, ruthless Governor General of occupied Polish territories and responsible for the death and displacement of Polish Jews, Poles and Slavs, was sentenced by the International Military Tribunal in Nüremberg and hanged in 1946.

Ferdinand Aus der Fünten, SS Commander in occupied Holland, received a death sentence; sentence later commuted to life in prison.

Irma Grese, SS woman administrator in Auschwitz and Bergen-Belsen, condemned to death by a British court, was executed in 1945.

Heinz Guderian, Commander of Panzer Group 3 and Chief of General Staff, credited with originating armored warfare, lives in retirement.

Heinrich Himmler, Reichsfuehrer SS and chief of police and Gestapo, committed suicide upon capture by the British at Lüneburg, May 23, 1945.

Rudolf Hoess, Commandant at Auschwitz, was condemned to death by a Russian court in Warsaw in 1947.

Ewald von Kleist, Commander of Panzer Group 1 and Army Group South, reportedly died in Russia.

Günther von Kluge, Commander of Army Group Center, committed suicide in 1944.

Josef Kramer, Commandant at Birkenau, later at Bergen-Belsen, was condemned to death by a British court at Lüneburg and executed in 1945.

Georg von Küchler, Commander of the XVIII Army and of Army Group North, was sentenced to 20 years in prison, sentence reduced to 12.

Wilhelm von Leeb, Commander of Army Group North, was sentenced to three years imprisonment.

Maria Mandel, SS woman at Auschwitz and Bergen-Belsen, was presumably captured and sentenced by the British.

Josef Mengele, camp doctor in Auschwitz who made the selections, fled to Argentina and later to Brazil; he presumably died there in 1978.

Vidkun Quisling, the Norwegian Minister during the German occupation, was sentenced to death by his own countrymen and executed in October 1945.

Hans Albin Rauter, Commander of the SS and police in Holland, was tried in The Hague, executed there in March 1949.

Walter von Reichenau, Commander of Army Group South, was freed and pensioned in 1951, died in 1953.

Gerd von Rundstedt, Commander of Army Group South, was freed and pensioned in 1951. Died in 1953.

Artur Seyss-Inquart, Reichskommissar for occupied Holland, was tried by the International Military Tribunal as a major war criminal and hanged in October 1946.

Heinrich von Stülpnagel, Commander of the XVIIth Army and Military Commander of France, was executed in 1944.

Otto von Stülpnagel, his successor as Military Commander in France, was arrested at Liberation and imprisoned; committed suicide in 1948.

Dome Sztojay, Prime Minister of Hungary during the German occupation, was executed there in 1946.

Sources

Works Consulted

Adler, H.G. *Theresienstadt, 1941-1954*. Tubingen, 1960.

Barber, Noel. *The Week France Fell*. New York: Stein and Day, 1976.

Bauer, Yehuda. *The Holocaust in Historical Perspective*. Seattle: University of Washington Press, 1978.

Cargill, Morris, ed. *A Gallery of Nazis*. New Jersey: Lyle Stuart, 1978.

Cavendish, Marshall, ed. *History of the Second World War*. pts. 1, 4, 7, 17. U.S.A., London: Marshall Cavendish, 1973.

Dawidowicz, Lucy S. *A Holocaust Reader*. New York: Behrman House, Inc., 1976.

Encyclopedia of the Holocaust, Israel Gutman, ed. New York: MacMillan, 1990. 4 vols.

Fest, Joachim C. *The Face of the Third Reich*. New York: Pantheon Books, 1970.

Gilbert, Martin. *The Holocaust*. New York: Hill and Wang, 1978.

Hayes, Paul M. *Quisling*. Bloomington: Indiana University Press, 1972.

Hilberg, Raul. *The Destruction of the European Jews*. Chicago: Quadrangle Books, 1961.

──────────. *Die Vernichtung der Europäischen Juden*. Berlin: Olle & Wolter, 1982.

Holt, John B. *Under the Swastika*. Chapel Hill: The University of North Carolina Press, 1963.

Kulski, Julian Eugeniusz. *Dying, We Live*. New York: Holt, Rinehart, and Winston, 1979.

Lederer, Zdenek. *Ghetto Theresienstadt*. London: E. Goldston, 1953.

Maass, Walter. *The Netherlands at War: 1940-1945*. New York: Abelard-Schuman, 1970.

Mau, Herman and Helmut Krausnick. *German History 1933-45*. London: Oswald Wolff (Pub.) Ltd., 1962.

Melzer, Milton. *Never To Forget: the Jews of the Holocaust*. New York: Harper and Row, 1976.

Michaelis, Meir. *Mussolini and the Jews*. Oxford: The Clarendon Press, 1978.

Mitchell, B.R. *European Historical Statistics from 1750-1970*. New York: Columbia University Press, 1975.

Oakley, Stewart. *A Short History of Denmark*. New York: Praeger Pub., 1972.

Petrow, Richard. *The Bitter Years: the Invasion and Occupation of Denmark and Norway, April 1940-May 1945*. New York: William Morrow and Co., Inc., 1974.

Reitlinger, Gerald. *The Final Solution*. New York: A.S. Barnes, 1961.

Robinson, Jacob. *The Holocaust and After: Sources and Literature in English*. Jerusalem: Israel University Press, 1973.

Roussy de Sales, Count Raoul De, ed. *My New Order*. Reynal and Hitchcock, 1941. (The Speeches of Hitler, 1922-1941).

Shirer, William. *The Rise and Fall of the Third Reich*. New York: Simon and Schuster, 1960.

Smith, Bradley F. *Reaching Judgment at Nüremberg*. New York: Basic Books, 1977.

Snyder, Louis Leo. *Documents of German History*. New York: Rutgers University Press, 1958.

_____. *Encyclopedia of the Third Reich*. New York: McGraw-Hill, 1976.

_____. *The War: a Concise History, 1939-45*. New York: Simon and Schuster, 1960.

Thomas, John Oram. *The Giant-Killers: the Story of the Danish Resistance Movement*, 1940-45. New York: Taplinger Publ., 1975.

Timetables of History: A Horizontal Linkage of People & Events, Bernard Grun, ed. 3rd, rev. ed. New York: Simon and Schuster, 1991.

Woodhouse, C.M. *The Struggle for Greece, 1941-1949*. New York: Beek-man/Esanu Pub., 1976.

Zisenwine, David W., ed. *Anti-Semitism in Europe: Sources of the Holocaust*. New York: Behrman House Inc., 1976.

Documentary Material

General Record of the Department of State; Decimal File 1945-49. From: 840.48 FAA/1-145 to 840.48 Refugees/2-2845.

Nazi Conspiracy and Aggression 10 vols. Washington: U.S. Government Printing Office, 1946.

Trials of War Criminals before the Nüremberg Military Tribunal. 15 vols. Washington: U.S. Government Printing Office, 1951-52.

Map Citation

All maps used are from the Cartographic Department of the National Archives, Washington, D.C.

Record Group 160, Record of the Armed Service Forces, NEWSMAP, Monday, October 18, 1943 (vol. II no. 26) week of October 7-October 14; 21st week of the war - 96th week of U.S. participation.

Newsmaps: September 11, 1944
November 6, 1944 (2 Maps)
May 15, 1944
April 3, 1944

Demographic statistics are from B.R. Mitchell, *European Historical Statistics from 1750-1950*. Columbia University Press, 1975.

For statistics pertaining to the Jews in Europe, I relied on Raul Hilberg, *The Destruction of the European Jews*, Quadrangle Books, 1961.

Military facts are from *The West Point Atlas of American Wars*, vol 2, Vincent J. Esposito, ed. Praeger, 1959.

For demographic details for European countries, I consulted the United States Government Printing Office's *Area Handbooks, 1971-1976*.

For geographic features for European countries, *The National Geographic Atlas of the World*, 4th ed., 1975, was used.

The World Highlights were culled from *Timetables of History: A Horizontal Linkage of People & Events*, 3rd, rev. ed., by Bernard Grun. New York: Simon and Schuster, 1991.

The Testimonies of Survivors and Victims

For my own story I was able to reenforce memory with the notes I wrote down after my liberation, in March 1945, while names, dates and events were still fresh. Copies of these notes are on file at the National Archives in Washington, D.C. and at the Leo Baeck Institute in New York.

Janusz Korczak's tragic destiny is garnered from *Ghetto Diary* by Janucz Korczak, published by Holocaust Library, New York, 1978.

Leesha's story of valor and resistance is culled from her book *The Tulips Are Red* by Leesha Rose, published by A.S. Barnes and Co., South Brunswick and New York, 1978.

Young Moshe Flinker's sorrowful fate is a summary of his diary, *The Spiritual Torment of a Jewish Boy in Nazi Europe* published by Yad Vashem, Jerusalem, 1972; translated from the original Hebrew entitled *Hana'ar Yomano shel Moshe Flinker* published by Yad Vashem in 1958.

Fania's experiences in Auschwitz are from her autobiography *Playing For Time*, translated by Judith Landry, published by Michael Joseph Ltd. and Atheneum Publishers, 1977; first published in France under the title *Sursis Pour L'Orchestre* published by Opera Mundi, Paris, 1976.

Alys Stanké's recollections are a recapitulation of his book *So Much To Forget: a Child's Vision of Hell*, by Alain Stanké, published by Gage Publishing, 1977.

Bryna's ordeal is a condensation of her story *The Vapor* by Bryna Bar Oni, published by Visual Impact, Inc., 1976.

Isabella Katz's remembrance of the Death March is a small part of the whole of her suffering as depicted in *Fragments of Isabella: a Memoir of Auschwitz*, by Isabella Leitner, published by Thomas Y. Crowell, 1978.

Index

A Note on the Design

The cover: The Hebrew letters on the cover are the Jewish names of those members of Gerda Haas's family and her husband's family who perished in the Holocaust: Her mother, Breindl bas Gabriel; her sister, Chava bas Yisroel; her husband's sisters Breindl bas Yehuda Halevi and Chava bas Yehuda Halevi

The Phoenix on the back cover: Gerda will always treasure the phoenix carved out of yellow metal that her friend Jirca gave her in Theresienstadt. She didn't dare wear it there, but once she was free she wore with pride and sadness. Although Jirca was dead, to Gerda it remains a symbol of hope, rebirth, and joy, the mythical bird lifting its proud neck from the depths of despair.

Photo Acknowledgements

pp. 33–41, Gerda Haas; p. 42. National Archives (W+C 981); p. 43, National Archives (W+C 982); p. 44 (top), National Archives (W+C 991), (bottom) UPI/Bettmann; pp. 45, 84 (bottom), 87, U.S. Army; p. 46, Bildarchiv Preussischer Kulturbesitz; p. 47, National Archives (W+C 990); p. 48, National Archives (W+C 998); p. 81, National Archives (W+C 746); pp. 82, 84 (top) courtesy of YIVO Institute for Jewish Research; p. 83, National Archives (Am.Im. 158); p. 85, Imperial War Museum; p. 86, National Archives (W+C 909); p. 88 National Archives (W+C 1075); p. 89, National Archives (W+C 1094); pp. 90, 92 (bottom) Library of Congress; p. 91, National Archives (W+C 990); p. 92 (top), National Archives (W+C 1104); p. 93 Independent Picture Service; pp. 94–95, National Archives (208-AA-206K-17); p. 96, Cleveland Public Library.